LISTENING AND SPEAKING

FOR JOB AND PERSONAL USE

L. Ann Masters, Administrator

Curriculum and Instructional Program Improvement Unit
Nebraska Department of Education
Lincoln, Nebraska

Merle Wood

Education Consultant
Formerly of Oakland Public Schools
Lafayette, California

South-Western Publishing Co.

Acquisitions Editor: Karen Schneiter
Series Editor: Mark Linton
Production Editor: Thomas N. Lewis
Associate Director/Design: Darren K. Wright
Associate Photo Editor/Stylist: Kimberly A. Larson
Associate Director/Photography: Diana W. Fleming
Assistant Photographer: Mimi Ostendorf
Marketing Manager: Shelly Battenfield

South-Western Publishing Co. gratefully acknowledges the foresight and commitment that Ben Willard, Acquisitions Editor, gave to this LIFE Series.

ISBN: 0-538-70568-X

Library of Congress Catalog Card Number: 91-60692

2 3 4 5 6 7 8 9 DH 9 8 7 6 5 4 3

Printed in the United States of America

Library of Congress Cataloging-in-Publication Data

Masters, L. Ann.
Listening and speaking for job and personal use / L. Ann Masters, Merle Wood.
p. cm.
Includes index.
ISBN 0-538-70568-X (pbk.)
1. Oral communication. I. Wood, Merle W. II. Title.
P95.M34 1992
302.2'242--dc20 91-60692
CIP

PREFACE

Basic skills are required for each of us to conduct our personal and business dealings. An increasing need exists to provide adults with these basic skills so they can improve both their personal interactions and employment opportunities.

As a result, the LIFE Series was developed because South-Western believes that Learning Is For Everyone (LIFE). The LIFE Series is specifically designed to provide adults with the basic skills needed for personal dealings and for job opportunities.

THE LIFE SERIES

The LIFE Series is a self-paced, competency-based program specifically designed for adults to develop basic skills for job and personal use. Each book in the Series provides interesting material, realistic examples, practical applications, and flexible instruction to promote learner success and self-confidence.

The LIFE Series is divided into three basic skill areas—communication skills, math skills, and life skills. LISTENING AND SPEAKING FOR JOB AND PERSONAL USE is one of the communication skills books in the LIFE Series. Each text-workbook is complete and may be used individually or in a series. The following is a complete list of the LIFE Series.

Communication Skills

- Spelling for Job and Personal Use
- Reading for Job and Personal Use
- Grammar and Writing for Job and Personal Use
- Punctuation, Capitalization, and Handwriting for Job and Personal Use
- Listening and Speaking for Job and Personal Use

Math Skills

- Basic Math for Job and Personal Use
- Decimals, Fractions, and Percentages for Job and Personal Use
- Calculator Math for Job and Personal Use

Life Skills

- Career Planning and Development
- Problem Solving and Decision Making
- Self-Esteem and Getting Ahead
- Money Management
- Finding and Holding a Job

STRUCTURE AND ORGANIZATION

Each book in the LIFE Series has the same appearance and structure enabling learners to experience more success and gain self-confidence as they progress. Competency-based instruction is also used throughout by first presenting clear objectives followed by short segments of material with specific exercises for immediate reinforcement.

The organization of LISTENING AND SPEAKING FOR JOB AND PERSONAL USE emphasizes good listening and speaking habits. In Part One, "Taking a Look at Listening and Speaking," students are introduced to the terminology related to the roles of listener and the speaker. The focus of Part Two, "Listening and Speaking in the Workplace," is on the best listening and speaking techniques to use on the job. In Part Three, "Personal Listening and Speaking Skills," the common listening and speaking experiences of everyday life are discussed, and the best techniques are reviewed.

The Glossary, Index, Answers, and Personal Progress Record at the end of LISTENING AND SPEAKING FOR JOB AND PERSONAL USE are designed to facilitate and enhance independent student learning and achievement.

SPECIAL FEATURES OF LISTENING AND SPEAKING FOR JOB AND PERSONAL USE

LISTENING AND SPEAKING FOR JOB AND PERSONAL USE is a complete and comprehensive package providing the student with learning material written specifically to meet the unique needs of the adult learner and providing the instructor with support materials to facilitate student success. Some special features include the following:

Design Characteristics

Each text-workbook in the LIFE Series, including LISTENING AND SPEAKING FOR JOB AND PERSONAL USE, uses a larger typeface to make it easier for the student to use and to read.

Appropriate Content

Real-life issues and skills are emphasized throughout the text with relevant examples and illustrations provided to which the student can relate.

Objectives

Instructional objectives are clearly stated for each unit letting students know what they will learn.

Checkpoints

Checkpoints follow short segments of instruction and provide students with an opportunity to immediately use what they have just learned.

Goals

Goals are listed for each exercise to give the student motivation and direction.

Study Breaks

Each unit contains study breaks that provide a refreshing break from study and yet contribute to the global literacy goal of the student.

Summaries

A summary of the student's accomplishments is provided at the end of each unit providing encouragement and reinforcement.

Putting It Together

The end-of-unit activities cover the theory presented in the Checkpoints and provide goals for students to measure their own skill development and success.

Glossary

Important terms in the text are printed in bold and defined the first time they are used. These terms are listed and defined in the Glossary for easy reference.

Answers

Answers for all the Checkpoints and Activities are provided at the back of the text-workbook and designed for easy reference to facilitate independent and self-paced learning.

Personal Progress Record

Students keep track of their own progress by recording scores on a Personal Progress Record. Students can measure their own success by comparing their scores to evaluation guides provided for each unit. Whenever a student's total score for a unit is below the minimum requirement, the student may request a Bonus Exercise from the instructor.

SPECIAL FEATURES OF THE INSTRUCTOR'S MANUAL

The Instructor's Manual provides general instructional strategies and specific teaching suggestions for LISTENING AND

SPEAKING FOR JOB AND PERSONAL USE along with supplementary bonus exercises and answers, testing materials, and a certificate of completion.

Bonus Exercises

Second-chance exercises for all activities are offered through bonus exercises provided in the Instructor's Manual. These bonus exercises enable instructors to provide additional applications to those students whose scores are less than desirable for a unit. Answers to all bonus exercises are also provided and can be duplicated for student use.

Testing Materials

Four assessment tools, entitled "Checking What You Know," are provided for this text. These tests may be used interchangeably as pretests or post-tests allowing for flexible use.

Certificate of Completion

Upon completion of each part of LISTENING AND SPEAKING FOR JOB AND PERSONAL USE, a student's success is recognized through a certificate of completion. This certificate has a listing of topics that were covered in this text. A master certificate is included in the manual.

LISTENING AND SPEAKING FOR JOB AND PERSONAL USE is designed specifically to help you invest in your adult learners' futures and to meet your instructional needs.

CONTENTS

ACKNOWLEDGMENTS

For permission to reproduce the photographs on the pages indicated, acknowledgment is made to the following:

UNIT 1 p. 9: Best Western International, Inc.

GETTING ACQUAINTED

Communication takes a big part of our time. Much of this is in the form of listening and speaking. The scene in Illustration GA-1 might be familiar to you.

Listening and speaking skills are important to your success in life. If you feel that you have problems with listening and speaking, you are not alone. Even a person with a university education often has some difficulty with listening and speaking skills. But studying and reviewing the keys to good listening and speaking can improve your communication skills.

While it may not seem entirely fair, an individual's listening and speaking ability reflects on the image that other people have of him or her. Because these skills are a part of our communication skill, our listening and speaking skills can even affect the kind of job that each of us is able to get and hold. Listening and speaking skills are required on almost every job today, as is suggested in Illustration GA-1.

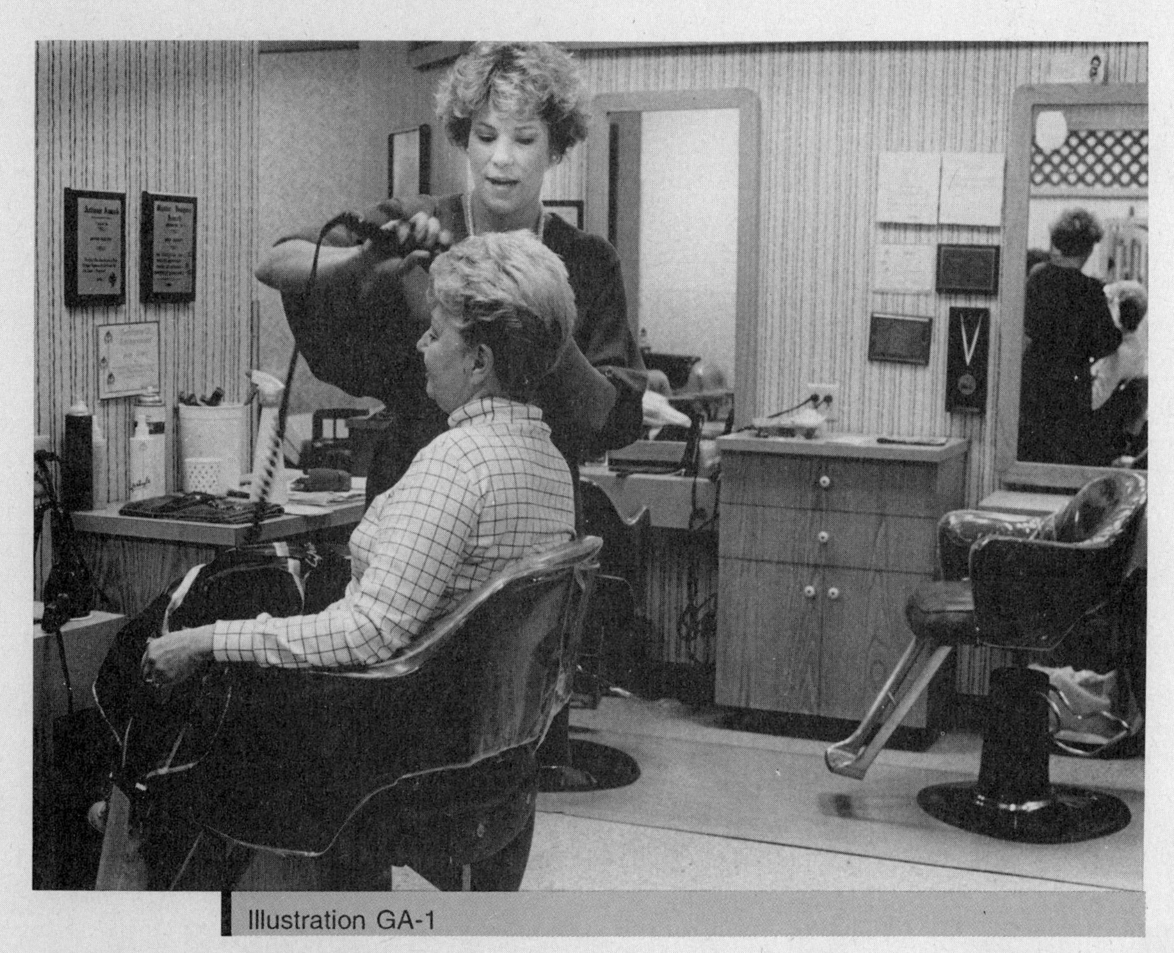

Illustration GA-1

No matter what your job is, listening and speaking skills are important.

You may be taking this listening and speaking program because you know your skills need improvement. Or you might be from a country where English is not spoken. If English is not your native language, you may see the need to develop skill in speaking and listening to the English language. Regardless of the reason for deciding to improve these important skills, this book should help you become a better communicator.

HOW YOU WILL LEARN

There is a system used in LISTENING AND SPEAKING FOR JOB AND PERSONAL USE to help you learn. You need to know how this system works.

Learn at Your Own Pace

You will progress through the lessons in LISTENING AND SPEAKING FOR JOB AND PERSONAL USE on your own. You can move ahead faster or go slower than other students. But don't be concerned about this. You are to work at *your* best speed.

Learn Skills Successfully

You are given learning objectives and goals. You will know what you are to accomplish. You will study a topic. Then you will practice what you have learned. When you have shown that you know the topic, you will move on to the next topic. If you have not learned the topic, you will do added study on that section. You will know just how well you are doing as you move through each step in this book.

Bonus Exercises

You may not reach your assigned goal on every practice activity. When this happens, you are asked to review the lesson again and then do a Bonus Exercise. The Bonus Exercises cover the same lesson as the practice activities in the book. They give you a second chance to reach your goal. Your instructor has copies of the Bonus Exercises.

Check Your Own Success

You will keep track of your own success. After completing each activity, you will check your own work. The answers are in the back of the book. Then you will record your score on your own Personal Progress Record. Your record is at the back of the book.

WHAT YOU WILL LEARN

As you study LISTENING AND SPEAKING FOR JOB AND PERSONAL USE, you will learn the basic skills needed for good listening and speaking. You will also have the opportunity to use these valuable skills. To achieve these goals, you will study three parts:

Part One	Taking a Look at Listening and Communicating
Part Two	Listening and Speaking in the Workplace
Part Three	Personal Listening and Speaking Skills

Taking a Look at Listening and Communicating

Your ability to understand the basic skills of listening and speaking is important to your ability to communicate. In Part One, you will learn the parts of the circle of communication.

Listening and Speaking in the Workplace

Part Two presents the situations in the workplace where your listening and speaking skills will need to be sharp. This information should help you feel more confident about your abilities to communicate in the workplace.

Personal Listening and Speaking Skills

In Part Three, you will study the listening and speaking skills important in your personal life. By knowing these skills well, you will be able to communicate comfortably and successfully.

SPECIAL FEATURES

LISTENING AND SPEAKING FOR JOB AND PERSONAL USE has a number of special features. These features will help you learn and apply the material successfully.

What You Will Learn

The goals you will accomplish by studying each unit are found at the beginning of the unit. These goals are labeled "What You Will Learn."

Checkpoints

This book has a number of exercises in the units called "Checkpoints." Each Checkpoint will help you check your understanding of a topic before moving on to the next topic.

Putting It Together

At the end of the units, you will find a section called "Putting It Together." This section contains several Activities. These are similar to the Checkpoints within the units. They will help you to apply and reinforce the skills you learned in the unit.

Making It Work

At the end of each part of the book, you will have the opportunity to review the information presented in the units of that part. This review will be another chance to check your knowledge.

Bonus Checkpoints and Activities

If you do not reach the assigned goal for any of the Checkpoints or Activities, you are asked to review the unit. Then you are asked to do a Bonus Checkpoint or Bonus Activity. These Bonus Exercises give you a second chance to succeed. These second-chance activities are not in this book. Your instructor has copies for you. Your instructor also has the answer key to these activities. You will use it to check your own work.

Answers

Answers to all the exercises and activities are provided in the back of this book. The answer pages are color-tinted, making them easy to find and use. You will use these pages to check your own work. Always do the exercises and activities *before* you look at the answers. Use the answers as a tool to verify your work—not as a means of completing the activities.

Personal Progress Record

You will check most of your work with the answers. Then you will record your score on your own Personal Progress Record located at the back of the book. After you complete a unit, you will be able to determine your level of success.

Completion Certificate

When you finish your study of *Listening and Speaking for Job and Personal Use,* you will be eligible for a certificate of completion. Your instructor will explain to you the skill level required for this award.

READY TO START

You are now ready to start improving your listening and speaking skills. Throughout this book, you will be given added directions. Through the guided study, completion of the Checkpoints and Activities, you will have an improved ability to communicate with others.

Your new and improved skills will prove to be of benefit to you. You can do your on-the-job communicating with added confidence. You will have improved opportunity to move up the job ladder, where—in many cases—well-developed listening and speaking skills are required.

PART ONE
TAKING A LOOK AT LISTENING AND COMMUNICATING

UNIT 1
SPEAKING AND COMMUNICATING WITH OTHERS

UNIT 2
ZEROING IN ON LISTENING

UNIT 3
SPECIAL LISTENING SKILLS

UNIT 1
SPEAKING AND COMMUNICATING WITH OTHERS

WHAT YOU WILL LEARN

When you finish this unit, you will be able to:

- Define communication.
- Explain the role of the listener in the communicating process.
- Explain the role of the sender in the communicating process.
- List examples of verbal and nonverbal messages.
- Describe the feedback process.
- Explain the circle of communication.

COMMUNICATING

You probably enjoy some of these speaking and listening situations everyday—listening to the radio, talking with a friend or neighbor, listening to the sound of a bird, or giving directions to a stranger. All of these activities are called *communicating.*

What Is Communication?

Communication is the process of sending and receiving information.

The process of sending and receiving information is called **communication**. You are continually involved in communication. If you ask a friend to help lift a heavy box and the friend helps you, you are communicating. If your neighbor asks you for a ride, and you say "sure," you are communicating.

What Is a Message?

A message is the item of communication being sent or received.

The item of communication that you are sending or receiving is known as the **message**. Communication transfers a thought or idea from the sender to the receiver. Life would be boring and perhaps impossible without communication.

RECEIVER OR LISTENER

Part of communicating is what you hear. When you hear, you are receiving information. Therefore, you are called a *receiver* or *listener.* A listener or receiver accepts information.

Illustration 1-1

Communication Process.

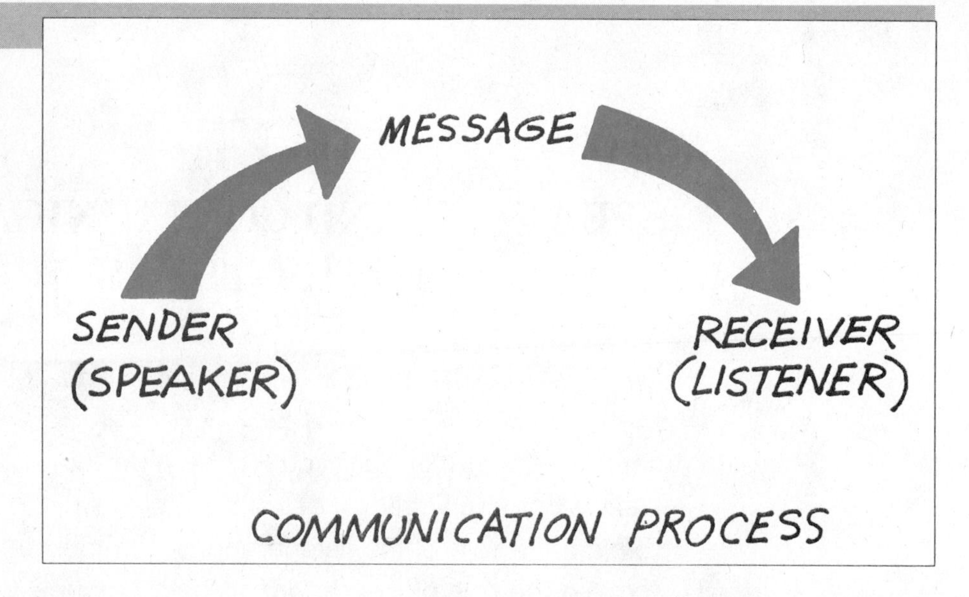

What Do You Hear?

Each day of your life you listen or receive information. You listen to the radio or a television set. You listen to the noises of the city—the sounds of cars, the voices of people passing you on the street, the blare of a radio from a cruising car, the whistle of a police officer, or the scream of a siren from a fire truck. Or maybe you listen to the sounds of the country life—the whistle of the wind, the babble of a stream, the whinny of a horse, the song of a bird, or the voice of a bullfrog. Whatever your life style, you do a lot of listening.

What Do You Receive?

As you listen to others, and the sounds of the city or country, you are actually hearing or receiving. What you hear are the messages of communication. The messages give you information or direction, warn you of danger, alert you to the needs of others, or relax your mind. You may be able to think of other messages or sounds you hear within a day.

MESSAGES FROM OTHERS

That which we are capable of feeling, we are capable of saying.

—Cervantes

Speak, that I may see thee.

—Ben Johnson

Only the educated are free.

—Epictetus

CHECKPOINT 1–1

YOUR GOAL: Get 4 answers correct.

In the space provided, list two messages or sounds most often heard in the city. You will get 1 point for each blank completed.

1. ______________________________

2. ______________________________

In the space provided, list two messages or sounds you received from someone today. You will get 1 point for each blank completed.

1. ______________________________

2. ______________________________

In the space provided, list two messages or sounds you like to receive in the country. You will get 1 point for each blank completed.

1. ______________________________

2. ______________________________

☞ *Check your work. Record your score.*

SENDER OR SPEAKER

In your daily routine, you are not always the listener or receiver of a message. Many times, you have the opportunity to be the sender or speaker of a message. When you are in the role of the sender, you send a thought or idea to someone else. When that idea or thought is spoken or sent to someone else, you are a sender or speaker of a message.

What Do You Send?

As the speaker, you may send information. For example: "The grocery store is on Adams Street." "Your shoe is untied." "The bus stops here at 9:15 a.m." You may provide others with directions. You may attempt to talk others into agreeing with you. Sometimes you speak to praise or thank others. For example: "Thanks for your help." "Bob, your work on my house was great." As the speaker or sender, you may protect someone by providing a warning. "Watch out for that beam!" "The dog bites." "The bus is turning."

Illustration 1-2

Providing information—one duty of the sender.

CHECKPOINT 1–2

YOUR GOAL: Get 8 answers correct.

In the space provided, list four messages which give information that you have sent or may send today. You will receive 1 point for each information message.

1. ____________________
2. ____________________
3. ____________________
4. ____________________

In the space provided, list four warnings you have given today or in the past. You will receive one point for each warning.

1. ____________________
2. ____________________
3. ____________________
4. ____________________

In the space provided, write two directions you have given or plan to give today. You will receive one point for each direction.

1. ______________________________

2. ______________________________

☞ *Check your work. Record your score.*

How Do You Send?

As a speaker or sender, you usually send messages with your voice. The sound of your voice helps others understand what you say. A firm, loud voice helps the receiver of your message know you are serious. A soft, gentle voice tells your receiver you are sending a kind message.

KINDS OF MESSAGES

Messages are sent in many ways. The words "good morning" spoken to another indicate that you want someone to have a pleasant morning. You nod your head to send the message that someone was noticed. You point at the clock and indicate that time is important.

Verbal Messages

A verbal message is a message sen t with words.

When you say "good morning," "hi," or "goodbye," you use your voice. In many ways your voice is you. You are the only person who has just that voice. Your friends do not have to see you to recognize you. All they have to do is hear your voice. When you use your voice to send a message, this is called a **verbal message.** An example of a verbal message might be: "Shut the door." "I hope you are feeling better." "I enjoyed the movie."

Nonverbal Messages

A nonverbal message is a message sent without words.

You may choose to send a message by an action. No spoken words are required. A message sent without using words is a **nonverbal message.**

You may wave to someone entering your work area. This physical action signals to your co-worker that you are saying "hello." No words were necessary. A neighbor may look at you and roll his or her eyes. This action sent you a message. What was it? Keep in mind the old saying, "Actions speak louder than words." If your words give one message and your nonverbal message gives another, the nonverbal message is stronger.

CHECKPOINT 1–3

YOUR GOAL: Get 3 answers correct.

In the left column are five common actions. In the space provided in the right column, write the message you would receive from the nonverbal message. You will receive 1 point for each nonverbal message described.

1. The tapping of a pencil. ________________
2. A tight fist raised above the head. ________________
3. The tapping of a foot. ________________
4. Crossing the arms on the chest. ________________
5. Pointing a finger. ________________

☞ ***Check your work. Record your score.***

Share your answers with others. Are your answers the same? There may be some differences. Nonverbal messages can easily be misunderstood.

CHECK MESSAGES

How can you be sure that the message you send is correctly received? How do you know if your co-worker thinks the joke you told is funny? How can you tell if your boss believes your excuse for being a few minutes late? How do you know if your friend likes your new shoes? How do you know if your sister shares your feeling that the temperature is too warm?

Watch the Listener

In order to check your message, you should watch the actions of the receiver. The actions of the receiver usually tell you how accurately the message has been received. If you tell a co-worker a joke and the reaction is laughter, you can assume the co-worker "got the joke" and thought it was funny.

> **MESSAGES FROM OTHERS**
>
> When in doubt, tell the truth.
>
> —Mark Twain
>
> No man pleases by silence; many please by speaking briefly.
>
> —Ausonius

Illustration 1-3

Keep your eye on the receiver.

What Are the Actions Called?

Feedback is the listener's response that tells the sender if the message is understood.

The actions of the receiver of a message are called **feedback.** You arrive at work five minutes late and tell your boss you were caught in traffic. The boss responds with a quick up and down nod and walks off. The feedback indicates that your explanation was accepted. You ask a friend, "How do you like my new shoes?" The feedback is "They look great," and the friend nods his or her head. You know your friend understood the question and likes your shoes. Remember, feedback may come in the form of a verbal or nonverbal message.

Feedback is the listener's response that tells the sender if the message is understood.

After feedback is added to the communication process, it looks like Illustration 1-4. The sender sends a message. The message is "Get on the bus." The receiver receives the message, nods, and gets on the bus. The sender knows the message is complete because of the actions of the receiver.

THE CIRCLE OF COMMUNICATION

The circle of communication is not complete when the sender's message reaches the receiver. The circle is only complete when the receiver's feedback reaches the sender to end the process. Illustration 1-4 shows you how good communication is a two-way process.

> If you tell Fido, "Sit!" and Fido doesn't sit, the circle of communication is not complete between you and Fido. Fido did not receive the message. You will need to try again.

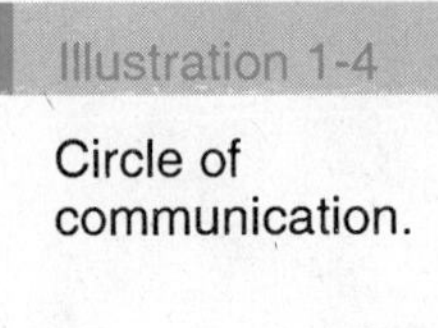

Illustration 1-4

Circle of communication.

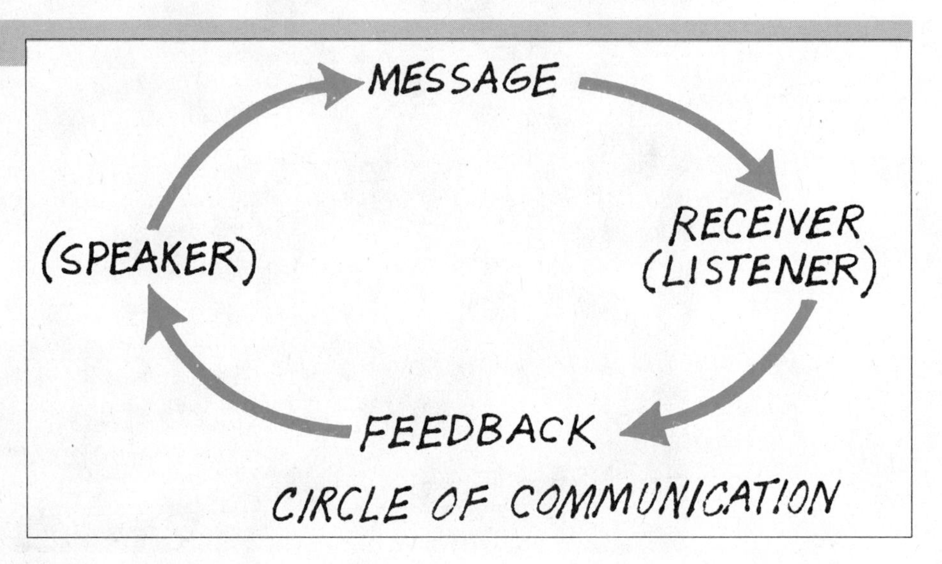

The channel is the route that a message takes to get to the receiver.

Senses that Help Complete the Circle

People use their senses as well as words to complete the circle of communication. The senses can help the two-way process. The route that a message takes to get to the receiver is called the **channel**. Sound waves are the channel related to the sense of hearing when verbal messages are sent. The sense of sight is involved with the channel through which visual (sight) messages are sent. If the sense of touch is used, the channel is the skin.

> If Fido doesn't sit after the sound-wave message is sent, you may want to try again using another channel. Try the touch channel this time. Place your hand on Fido's rump and push down. If Fido sits, you know the circle of communication is complete.

Additional Senses

Many times you will use more than one of your senses to help get a message across. For example, you say to a person, "I'm sorry you are feeling ill." You have used the verbal channel to send your message. To add additional meaning to your message, you squeeze the hand of the person. You have added the touch channel. The receiver of the message squeezes your hand, and you know the message was communicated.

CHECKPOINT 1–4

YOUR GOAL: Get all 3 answers correct.

Place an X in the space provided for the channel of communication which will be used to complete the communication process in these examples. Give yourself 1 point for each correct answer.

	Sight	Sound	Touch
• A teacher determines that Arthur wants to answer a question.	X		
1. Business people greet each other with a handshake.			
2. Dad feels the head of a child after the child complains of a headache.			
3. Two friends talk on the phone.			

☞ ***Check your work. Record your score.***

WHAT YOU HAVE LEARNED

- The process of sending and receiving information is called communication.
- Receiving or listening is receiving and/or accepting information.
- Sending or speaking is sending a thought or idea to someone.
- Messages sent to others may be sent with words (verbal messages) or actions (nonverbal messages).
- Checking to see if your message has been received is done by observing the receiver.
- The actions of the receiver are feedback.
- The circle of communication is complete when the message has gone from the sender to the receiver and back to the sender.

PUTTING IT TOGETHER

ACTIVITY 1-1 YOUR GOAL: Get 3 answers correct.

Locate a cartoon in a local newspaper which shows an example of the circle of communication. Attach the cartoon to this page. Answer the question about your cartoon in the spaces provided. Give yourself 1 point for each correct anwer.

1. What is the message the sender wanted the listener to receive?

   ____

2. Was the message received correctly by the listener?

   ____

3. What additional words or nonverbal actions would have helped the speaker send the message?

   ____

4. What additional channels could the speaker have used to get the message across?

   ____

5. What signs of feedback do you see in the cartoon?

   ____

☞ ***Check your work. Record your score.***

ACTIVITY 1-2 YOUR GOAL: Get 5 answers correct.

In the space provided, list five nonverbal actions that you see in a single day. Watch for these actions on television and as you talk with and watch others. Give yourself 1 point for each correct answer.

- Scratching the head

1. ______________________________
2. ______________________________
3. ______________________________
4. ______________________________
5. ______________________________

☞ ***Check your work. Record your score.***

ACTIVITY 1-3 YOUR GOAL: Get 3 answers correct.

What message(s) would you receive in the following settings? No verbal messages are given in addition to what you are seeing. Write your answers in the spaces provided. Give yourself 1 point for each correct answer.

- A woman dressed in a beaded, long gown.

  The woman is going to a party. The woman is rich.

1. A man wearing a ski jacket has his leg in a cast.

   ____

   ____

2. A shivering woman on a park bench with a paper sack beside her.

   ____

   ____

3. A student slumped down in a desk.

   ____

   ____

4. A picture of the Statue of Liberty with fireworks in the background.

   ____

   ____

5. A woman with tears in her eyes walking out of a hospital.

   ____

   ____

☞ ***Check your work. Record your score.***

UNIT 2

ZEROING IN ON LISTENING

WHAT YOU WILL LEARN

When you finish this unit, you will be able to:

- Explain why not all hearing is listening.
- Describe the roadblocks to effective listening.
- Describe the types of listeners.
- Explain how to be an active listener.
- Explain how to be a listener who separates facts from opinions.

"I'M LISTENING, BUT I CAN'T HEAR YOU"

Have you had the experience of watching an entire television news program and after a few minutes you realize you remember nothing that has been said? Perhaps you have talked with a gabby friend on the phone and not truly listened. Were you embarrassed when your friend asked you a question and you couldn't answer? Can you listen to an ad on the radio and five minutes later not remember the product? If you have been in any of these situations, you may be hearing and not listening. As a listener, you hear and receive the message. Sometimes you may hear and not receive.

ROADBLOCKS TO LISTENING

Many roadblocks can stop you from receiving a message. You need to recognize these roadblocks. If you understand the roadblocks, you can begin to remove them. Then you can work on your listening skills. Roadblocks to listening are noise, poor attitude, thinking ahead, mind moving too fast, and lack of attention.

Noise

Too many sounds at one time can be a roadblock to listening. Noise is sound that interferes with listening.

CHECKPOINT 2–1

YOUR GOAL: Get 6 or more answers correct.

In the space provided, list all of the noises that you might hear at a church service. The first one is completed as an example. Give yourself 1 point for each answer you can think of.

- Coughing

1. ______________________
2. ______________________
3. ______________________
4. ______________________
5. ______________________
6. ______________________
7. ______________________
8. ______________________

☞ ***Check your work. Record your score.***

You will need to decide what you want to listen to. You will need to block out those noises that will interfere with the message you want to hear. For example, if you are in church and want to listen to the message of the choir, you will need to block out the other noises or sounds which you listed in Checkpoint 2–1.

Poor Attitude

Having a poor attitude can keep you from listening well. For example, if you think a conversation between two of your friends is boring, you stop listening. Your thoughts move to noise that is around you. You miss the conversation because you took on the attitude that it was unimportant. A poor attitude can be dangerous. You may miss important information.

Thinking Ahead

Two people are needed to have a conversation. If you are enjoying a conversation with a friend, you take turns speaking and listening. Sometimes you may take your turn for listening to think about your next speaking time. If this happens, you are hearing your friend's message but not listening to it. When you

MESSAGES FROM OTHERS

The reason why so few people are agreeable is that each is thinking more about what he intends to say than about what others are saying, and we never listen when we are eager to speak.

—LaRochefoucauld

reply, your words may not make sense because you did not listen to the words of your friend. He or she may have moved the conversation to a new topic and you missed it!

For example, what has happened in this conversation?

CHIEN: The weather is beautiful today.

AMY: Yes, it surely is a lovely day. I am going for a long walk in the park this afternoon. Have you heard anything about expansion of the park?

CHIEN: The temperature is going to reach 80 degrees today. The humidity is not to go above 20 percent.

Chien was thinking ahead to his next comment on the weather. He wasn't listening to Amy's statements about the park.

Mind Moving Too Fast

Most speakers talk at a rate of about 125 words a minute. Most listeners listen at a rate of about 500 words a minute. If you are listening at the normal rate of 500 words a minute, you are ahead of the speaker. Your mind can wander. You may begin to daydream. Your mind is off to other things, and you are going to miss the points of the speaker. If you get ahead of the speaker, use this valuable time to review what the speaker has said. Keep your mind on the speaker's comments as the listener does in Illustration 2-1.

Lack of Attention

Good listening requires that listeners keep their thoughts on what is being said. When you do not pay close attention to the speaker and his or her message, you cannot be listening. Not paying close attention to the message being said may be a costly mistake. For example, if you are listening to directions on the job and not paying close attention, you may do something wrong and cause injury or expense to your employer.

On the job, you must make the effort to pay attention. Paying attention will prevent you from missing important information. Paying attention will also help create a sense of good will with the speaker. Everyone likes to be listened to!

Illustration 2-1

Listening vs. speaking time.

CHECKPOINT 2–2

YOUR GOAL: Get 3 or more roadblocks correct.

In the space provided, list the roadblocks to listening without looking back in the text . Give yourself 1 point for each correct answer.

1. ______________________________
2. ______________________________
3. ______________________________
4. ______________________________
5. ______________________________

☞ ***Check your work. Record your score.***

KINDS OF POOR LISTENERS

By now you recognize that some people listen better than others. You know the roadblocks to listening. Let's take a look at the poor listeners.

Selfish Listener

Have you ever talked with someone who could hear things only the way he or she wanted to hear them? If you have, you have talked with a **selfish listener**. A selfish listener listens only

MESSAGES FROM OTHERS

The best kind of conversation is that which may be called thinking aloud.
—William Hazlitt

Nobody ever listened himself out of a job.
—Calvin Coolidge

Nature has given man one tongue and two ears, that we may hear twice as much as we speak.
—Epictetus

A selfish listener listens only to what he or she wants to hear as it relates to his or her wants, needs, or desires.

to what he or she wants to hear as it relates to his or her wants, needs, or views.

The selfish listener forgets that everyone says something worth listening to. The selfish listener thinks that few people can say anything of value. These listeners do not encourage speakers by showing an interest, and they are not offered interesting information. Therefore, the selfish listener is the loser. The selfish listener cheats himself or herself out of learning from others.

Lazy Listener

A lazy listener listens only enough to get by.

A **lazy listener** does not work to pay attention to what is being said. They listen to only what they feel must be heard to get by.

A lazy listener will often cut off a speaker with some negative remarks like, "Yeah, I know that." "OK, I've got it." "Spare me the details." Learn to recognize the lazy listeners' nonverbal messages as shown in Illustration 2-2. Lazy listeners will not move up the ladder of success because they do not take advantage of learning opportunities.

Emotional Listeners

An emotional listener is a person overwhelmed by feelings upon hearing a certain word or words.

Certain words may "set you off." When you hear a given word, you may become so angry that you hear nothing else. You have become emotional over a word or words. An **emotional listener** is overwhelmed by feelings. For example, a police officer may become so angry because he or she has been called a "pig" that he or she becomes emotionally deaf. This kind of deafness can also happen when you are "turned on" by certain words. Someone calls you a good-looking person, and you are so excited with the compliment that you hear nothing further.

Emotional listeners cannot listen effectively because they are caught up in a few words that trigger them. Don't let this happen to you. Forget the word(s) and allow your thoughts to move on with the conversation.

Illustration 2-2

Don't be a lazy listener!

CHECKPOINT 2–3

YOUR GOAL: Get 3 or more words.

In the space provided, list words that trigger you to extreme anger or happiness. You will receive 1 point for each listed "trigger word." The first one is completed as an example.

- **Communist**

1. __________
2. __________
3. __________
4. __________
5. __________

☞ ***Check your work. Record your score.***

Facts Listener

A facts listener is a person who does not want to hear background information or listen to any more information than necessary.

A **facts listener** does not want to hear background information or listen to any more information than necessary. Listeners who hear only the facts are likely to miss the point of information. Facts listeners fail to pay attention to the speaker's feelings, gestures, or suggestions. The facts listener is like the student who is only concerned about what is on the test. He or she is not concerned about learning.

Defensive Listener

A defensive listener is a person who is not willing to listen to anything that does not agree with his or her beliefs.

The **defensive listener** is similar to the selfish listener. The defensive listener is not willing to see things as others see them. If you are a defensive listener, you do not listen to anyone who does not agree with your beliefs and values. As a defensive listener, you seek only information that agrees with your needs and beliefs. You think that if anyone disagrees with you, he or she is attacking you. For example, if you feel that the sales tax in your state should not be increased, you refuse to listen to anyone who feels that the sales tax must go up. You will not listen to information that may explain what services the increase will provide for you. You feel that the speaker is attacking you as a person because he or she does not agree with your opinion on an increase in sales tax. The defensive listener cannot effectively listen or understand because he or she is not open to new ideas or thoughts.

CHECKPOINT 2–4

YOUR GOAL: Get all 5 remarks matched correctly.

Write the type of listener who would make the remarks in the space provided. The first one is completed as an example. You will receive 1 point for each correct answer.

Remark	Listener Type
• "Just the facts, ma'am. All we want are the facts."	Facts listener
1. "Don't say Communist to me."	______________
2. "Spare me the details."	______________
3. "I already have my own opinion on legalizing drugs."	______________
4. "Yeah, I've got it."	______________
5. "Have you heard one of the boss's pep talks yet? If you've heard one you've heard them all."	______________

☞ ***Check your work. Record your score.***

ACTIVE LISTENER

A good listener is an **active listener**. An active listener realizes the benefits of good listening. An active listener is willing to work hard at the skill of listening in order to learn from others.

MESSAGES FROM OTHERS

I know how to listen when clever men are talking. This is the secret of what you call my influence.

—Unknown

Why Be an Active Listener?

An active listener is willing to work hard at the skill of listening in order to learn from others.

If you are an active listener, you will have an advantage. You will receive more and better information. You will make better decisions. Your decisions will be based on information, opinions, and experience of others. You will show to others that you are mature because you are open to the thoughts of others.

Directions For Active Listening

You will find that it takes time and practice to be an active listener. What makes Dean a good listener in the following conversation?

DEAN: Judy, tell me how to get to the theater, and I'll meet you and Rosa there.

JUDY: OK. From here, go down Arthur Road to Adams Street.

DEAN: Do I go east or west on Arthur Road?

JUDY: Go east. When you get to Adams, go north. Walk about three blocks until you see Barth's Drug Store.

DEAN: Which side of the street is it on?

JUDY: The west side. Turn left on the street just after the drug store, and you'll see the theater.

DEAN: Check me. East on Arthur to Adams; north on Adams Street, left on the street just after the drug store.

JUDY: That will get you there. See you later!

Dean is an active listener. He asked questions during the conversation. By asking questions, he let Judy know that he was interested in her directions. He reviewed what he had heard with the speaker. Dean provided feedback so that the circle of communication was complete.

The following are directions on becoming an active listener:

1. *Take Time to Listen.* The first key to active listening is to agree to take time to listen to a message. Stop what you are doing—talking, working, daydreaming, or watching television. An active listener concentrates on the speaker's message.

2. *Help the Speaker.* Show the speaker that you are interested in what he or she is saying. Look at the speaker.

Indicate interest by nodding, frowning, or smiling at the right time to let the speaker know you are listening. Make brief comments or ask questions from time to time. “Go on!” “Great!” “Good for you.” “Then what happened?” The more you can get the speaker to share, the more you will learn.

3. *Get Rid of Noise.* Focus on listening to the speaker. Separate you and the speaker from outside noises as the two people in Illustration 2-3 are doing. Actively put away distractions. Turn off the television. Turn down the volume of the radio. Move away from the conversation of others. Turn off noisy machinery. Close a door.

4. *Write the Main Ideas.* Listening for main ideas will help you remember the main points of the message. You should get in the habit of writing down the main ideas in an outline form. Writing the main ideas or directions from your supervisor will help you avoid mistakes.

5. *Listen with an Open Mind.* An open mind is one that will listen to ideas and opinions with which you disagree. You are willing to hear the other side and learn. Opinions about the topic or the speaker get in the way of your listening and learning. Judge the speaker's message by what is said.

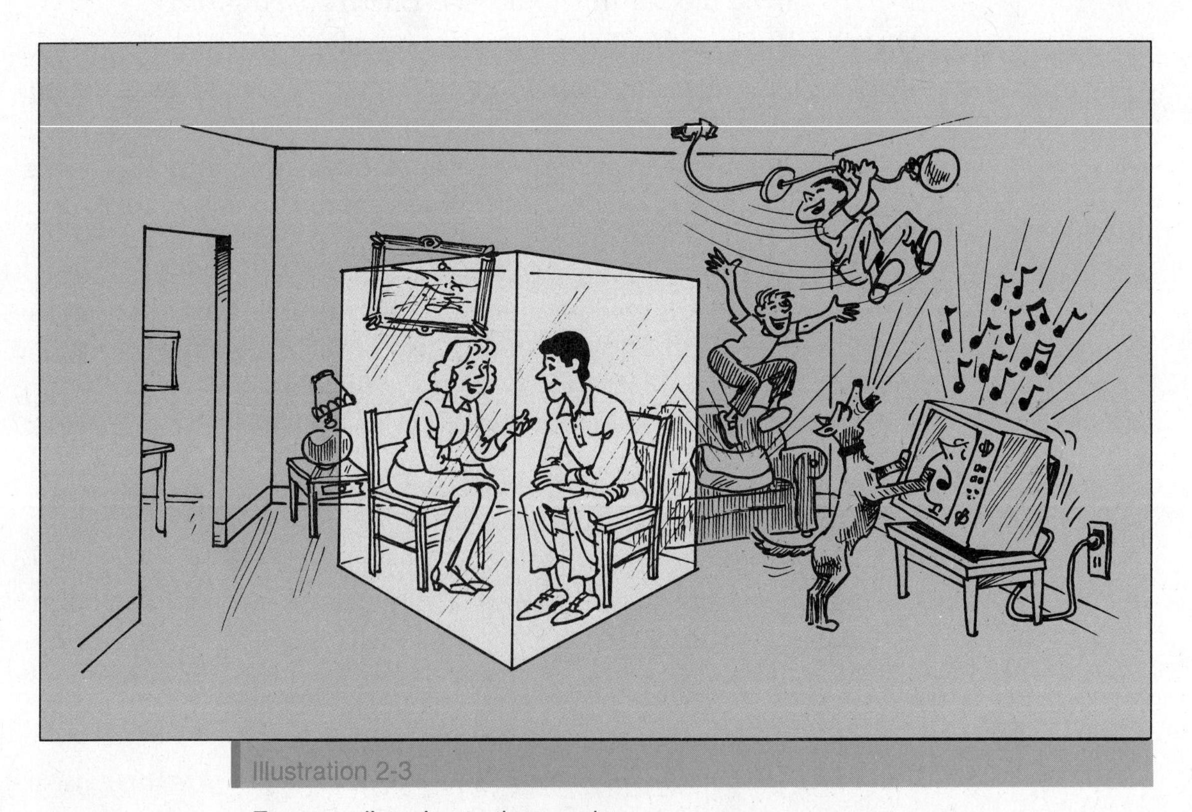

Illustration 2-3

Focus on listening to the speaker.

Disregard looks, actions, or personality. Attempt to understand the speaker's feelings. Respect the thoughts of others.

6. *Provide Feedback.* You should be prepared to question or comment when a speaker stops talking. Feedback will help you seek more information from the speaker. Asking questions or making comments also shows the speaker that you are listening. Watch the nonverbal feedback you give as you listen. Use eye contact, a smile, or a nod to let your speaker know you are an active listener. If you frown, yawn, or turn your eyes away, you are showing the speaker you are not interested. Nonverbal feedback from listeners is shown in Illustration 2-4.

Illustration 2-4

Watch your nonverbal feedback.

CRITICAL LISTENING

Critical listening is determining the acuracy of the message.

You will at times need to separate the main thoughts or facts from the opinions of others. You will need to do some **critical listening**. A critical listener listens to determine the accuracy of the message. You will need to think through the main ideas and details. You will need to measure the message by deciding what is fact and what is opinion.

Separate Main Thoughts from Details

You need to rely on your critical listening skills to help you sort information. Separate the main ideas from the details. Details help you understand the main thoughts. For example, you may listen to these directions on the job. "Take these letters to the shipping area. They came from the accounting department. Give the letters to Juanita Gonzalez. Juanita has been around for many years and will know where to put the letters. Go to lunch after you deliver the letters." All you need to know from this message is that the letters go to Juanita Gonzalez in the shipping area. Where the letters came from, how long she has been on the job, and a reminder to go to lunch are details.

Separate Fact from Opinion

As a critical listener, you will want to play detective. Your game will include separating facts from opinions. Separate that which can be proven, which are called "facts," from opinions. **Opinions** are what the speaker says based on his or her personal beliefs or feelings. Opinions may not always be based on fact. Critical listeners will work hard at separating facts from opinions. Facts and opinions are listed in Illustration 2-5. Study these lists to learn how to separate fact from opinion.

Illustration 2-5

Facts vs. opinions.

Facts	Opinions
—It's raining.	—Alaska is too cold.
—She wore a red dress.	—Her dress is too tight.
—It is 80 degrees.	—It is too hot.
—The car is blue.	—The car is pretty.
—The tank is full.	—The road is too rough.

WHAT YOU HAVE LEARNED

- You may hear sounds, noises, or messages without listening to them. Listening is hearing and receiving the message.
- The roadblocks to effective listening are: noise, poor attitude, thinking ahead, mind moving too fast, and lack of attention.
- The types of undesirable listeners are: selfish listeners, lazy listeners, emotional listeners, facts listeners, and defensive listeners.
- An effective listener is an active listener. The active listener takes time to listen, helps the speaker, gets rid of noise, listens for main ideas, listens with an open mind, and provides feedback.
- A critical listener listens to determine the accuracy of the message. The critical listener separates the facts from the speaker's opinions.

PUTTING IT TOGETHER

ACTIVITY 2–1 YOUR GOAL: Get 3 or more answers correct.

Read each of the following paragraphs. In the space provided, write the name of the listener roadblock being described. Give yourself 1 point for each correct answer.

1. Rex listened to his co-worker tell about how to lock the door at closing time. The co-worker talked on and on about the problems with the east door. Rex lost interest and didn't hear that there was a door to be locked on the west side of the building.

   Roadblock: ______________________________

2. Joey was talking with Mary. Mary was telling Joey about her new job at the packing plant. Joey was pleased for Mary, but he was thinking of how to tell Mary that he too had a new job.

   Roadblock: ______________________________

3. The radio station was telling listeners about how to keep spiders out of doors. Al thought to himself, "Let's get on with the music. Who cares about spiders."

   Roadblock: ______________________________

4. Alice wanted to listen to job openings announced on the radio. The baby was crying. The children next door were playing in the yard. A fire truck was screaming past.

   Roadblock: ______________________________

5. Fred was listening to the directions on how to fill out the form to request Social Security benefits. The person giving the directions was explaining the information needed on page 1. Fred felt he understood page 1 and was looking at pages 2 and 3.

   Roadblock: ______________________________

☞ *Check your work. Record you score.*

ACTIVITY 2–2 YOUR GOAL: Get all 5 answers correct.

In the space provided, write the type of listener being described. The first is completed as an example. Give yourself 1 point for each correct answer.

- Lazy listeners listen only to what they must to get by.

1. ______________________ listeners listen only to what they want to hear as it relates to their needs, wants, or views.

2. ______________________ listeners do not work hard to pay attention.

3. ______________________ listeners are quickly angered by certain words.

4. ______________________ listeners do not want to hear details or background information.

5. ______________________ listeners do not listen to information with which they do not agree.

☞ *Check your work. Record your score.*

ACTIVITY 2–3 YOUR GOAL: Get 4 or more answers correct.

Match the *acts* of active listening in Column A with the *keys* to active listening in Column B. Write the correct letter in the space provided. The first one is completed as an example. Give yourself 1 point for each correct answer.

Column A	Column B
• Nodding at the speaker.	___•___ Providing feedback.
A. Smiling at the speaker.	1. ______ Help the speaker.
B. Jotting down four or five thoughts of the speaker.	2. ______ Provide feedback.
C. Closing a door to get rid of sounds of the street.	3. ______ Listen with an open mind.
D. Putting yourself in the place of the speaker.	4. ______ Take time to listen.
E. Asking a question of the speaker.	5. ______ Listen for main ideas.
F. Stopping what you are doing.	6. ______ Get rid of noise.

☞ *Check your work. Record your score.*

ACTIVITY 2–4 YOUR GOAL: Get 3 or more answers correct.

Separate fact from opinion. Write "fact" in the space provided by each statement of fact. Write "opinion" in the space provided by each opinion statement. The first one is completed as an example. Give yourself 1 point for each correct answer.

• He carried a handgun. ___Fact___________________

1. Smith's Dairy was robbed. ________________________

2. Armed robbery is dangerous. ________________________

3. The police were too slow. ______________________

4. The robber wore a blue jacket. ______________________

5. The robber will be caught soon. ______________________

☞ ***Check your work. Record your score.***

UNIT 3

SPECIAL LISTENING SKILLS

WHAT YOU WILL LEARN

When you finish this unit, you will be able to:

- Apply the basic procedures of notetaking.
- Demonstrate how to take a message.
- Provide feedback to the speaker.

NOTETAKING

Notes are necessary when information is important enough to be remembered. Plan ahead. Take paper and pencil or pen to any situation where you know important information will be shared, or directions given. Notetaking can be particularly helpful in the workplace. Any meeting with your boss calls for notetaking. Keep all of your notes in the same notebook for easy reference.

Personal-use notes are also helpful. Keep a small note pad and a pen in your pocket or purse. Use them for taking down directions, telephone numbers, or other useful information, as the person shown in Illustration 3-1 is doing.

Notetaking is a good habit. You can refresh your memory with notes. There are several ways to take notes. You can write an outline or write a summary paragraph. You can divide a page to separate facts from ideas and questions.

Outline

Limit your notetaking to the main ideas. A listener who spends too much time taking notes may miss the heart of the message.

A sample of the right kind of notetaking follows. You attend a State Job Service meeting to get ideas for your next job application. The following is a part of the presentation:

> Let us assume that you have now completed the application blank. Look over your work before returning the application to the personnel office. Review each line of the appli-

Illustration 3-1

Don't leave home without a pad/pen.

cation to be sure that you have answered each question. Check to be sure that the dates of past jobs are accurate and complete. Be sure that you have signed and dated the application before returning it. The application is not valid without your signature. Smile when you turn in the application and say thank you.

What do you want to remember? The important points you want to remember can be outlined in three main points. Points I, II, and III could perhaps be shortened. You need only write enough to help you recall the main thoughts. Don't forget to put a date, time, and title on your notes.

```
8/23/—  State Job Service Workshop   2 p.m.
   I. Check to be sure all lines of application
      are filled out.
  II. Review the dates of past jobs for accuracy.
 III. Sign and date the application.
```

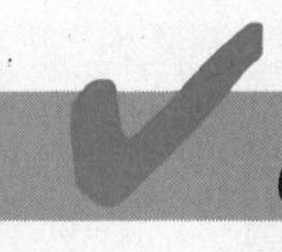

CHECKPOINT 3–1

YOUR GOAL: Get 2 or more main points of the presentation.

Read the following paragraphs. Outline the main points of the paragraphs in the space provided. Give yourself 1 point for each major point of the outline.

PROFESSIONAL FOOTBALL ON TELEVISION

Professional football has become very popular on television. Once, few people knew any professional football players by name. Now the big stars are known across the country. Professional football was once a minor sport. Now it is big business.

All three major networks carry professional football games. NBC carries games of the American Conference. CBS carries games of the National Conference. ABC carries Monday night games of both conferences.

Football is fun to watch on television. The game is exciting in the stadium. However, you can miss a lot of the action. On television, the camera follows the action closely. Announcers explain plays and tell why the players did what they did. Color television brings out the color of the uniforms and the stadium itself.

____

____

____

____

____

____

____

____

☞ ***Check your work. Record your score.***

MESSAGES FROM OTHERS

He listens well who takes notes.

—Dante Alighieri
1265–1321

The true art of memory is the art of attention.

—Samuel Johnson

Summary Paragraph

In some situations, taking notes may be difficult. You may not be prepared. Or taking notes may not be appropriate in some situations. If this happens to you, immediately summarize in a paragraph what was said. Date your notes. An example summary paragraph of the session at the State Job Service Workshop follows:

```
8/23/— State Job Service Workshop 2 p.m.
The State Job Service recommends that before
turning in an application blank it should be
reviewed. Check dates for accuracy. Be sure
all blanks are filled in. Sign and date the
application.
```

CHECKPOINT 3–2

YOUR GOAL: Write down 3 or more main points of the job.

Write a short summary paragraph in the space provided. Include the points to remember from the directions given by your boss. Give yourself 1 point for each statement you included in your paragraph.

> Your job is to spray the vegetables each morning at 9:00 a.m. Leave whatever other duties you are doing and spray the vegetables. The spray hoses are under the lettuce bin. Pull out the hose. Put the nozzle on position 2 for a fine mist. Spray until all are wet. If you have any questions about the amount of spraying necessary, ask Su-ling, the produce manager.

____

____

____

____

☞ ***Check your work. Record your score.***

Divided Page

Another way to take notes is to fold a sheet of paper the long way. Then, lay the paper flat so that you can use both sides of the fold. On the left side of the fold, list the facts as you hear them. Number each item. The right side of the page has a special purpose. Write down ideas that come to your mind as you are listening. Also, this is a place to jot down questions you may want to ask the message sender later. Always date your notes and give them a title. Illustration 3-2 shows how divided-page notes look.

Illustration 3-2

Divided-page notetaking.

Notes: State Job Service Workshop

Date: 8/23/--

Facts	Ideas
1. Review application	What color ink should I use?
2. Check date for accuracy	May I use a pencil?
3. Date and Sign	May I take the application home to complete?

CHECKPOINT 3–3

YOUR GOAL: Get 3 or more main points of the presentation.

Read the following information. Write a set of divided page notes in the space provided. Give yourself 1 point for each correct line of notes.

Consumers problems affect everybody. What can you do to become a better shopper? Here are some suggestions that will help you:

1. Don't be overwhelmed by advertising. Check the claims of the advertiser. Ask others about the products advertised.

2. Watch out for emotional, judgmental words. Expressions like *free*; *giant economy size*; *low, low prices*; and *bonus* are just a few. Very few products are really "free." A "bonus" usually requires a purchase that more than makes up for the bonus gift.

3. Check the labels of what you buy.

4. Read the contents of the food you buy.

5. Guard against your own weaknesses. Don't buy on the spur of the moment. Many shoppers come home with products they don't need. These items are often placed where everybody can easily see them. They may be near checkout counters. Candy is placed at a child's eye level. Shopper beware!

☞ ***Check your work. Record your score.***

Review Your Notes

Review your notes as soon as possible. Write out any shortened words that you used to save writing time. Correct any errors. Use different colored ink or pencil to highlight important points. If you have any questions about the information, this is the time to get them answered.

MESSAGE TAKING

There are two message situations where skillful and considerate listening is necessary. The first is when you take a message from a telephone call. The second is when you take a message from a face-to-face conversation.

Preparation for Taking a Message

Let the caller, friend, or visitor know that you are willing to take a message. Train yourself to ask the questions that will help you take a message. Some questions and phrases show a willingness to take messages. For example:

"May I tell Sheila you called?"
"Do you have a message for Hank?"

"Is there a number where you can be reached?"
"I will be glad to tell Lucia you called."

If you are talking to a friend, face-to-face, take time to write down the message for another friend. If a visitor comes to your door, ask him or her to wait until you get paper and pen or pencil to write down the message. Use a checklist in your mind like the one in Illustration 3-3 to be sure that all information is complete.

Illustration 3-3

Message checklist.

____ Who is the message for?
____ Who left the message?
____ What is the message?
____ What does the caller or visitor want you to leave in the message?
____ Who took the message? When?

Telephone Messages

Answering a telephone should be done with a "smile" in your voice. Keep a scratch pad and a pen or pencil near the telephone.

When the telephone rings, answer it promptly. Pick up the receiver on the first or second ring. If the call is for someone else, call the person to the telephone promptly. Do not shout into the receiver like the caller who blasted the person shown in Illustration 3-4.

Illustration 3-4

Answering the telephone.

If the person called is not available, offer to take a message. Then, write down the message. Asking the right questions is demonstrated in the following sample telephone conversation.

SAM: Hello!
CALLER: Hi, I would like to speak with Jane.
SAM: Jane is not available now. May I take a message and ask her to return your call?
CALLER: Yes, ask her to call me. (pause)
SAM: Your name please?
CALLER: Cristina Mendez.
SAM: What number shall I ask Jane to call?
CALLER: 555-8257. That number belongs to a neighbor who will call me to the phone.
SAM: I'll ask Jane to call Cristina Mendez at 555-8257 when she comes home from work.
CALLER: Thank you.

As the listener, you are responsible for asking questions to get the information for a message. In the sample telephone conversation, Sam asked the caller for for information to pass on to Jane. Repeat the information you receive to make sure that you relay correct information.

Message on a Form

In the workplace, telephone message forms are used to guide you in writing a message. A sample workplace message form is shown in Illustration 3-5.

Telephone Message

For A. J. Cronan From Armtek Int'l.

Would like you to call ☐ Left no message ☐

Returned your call ☐ Will call again ☒

Left the following message new representative wants to set up an appointment

Tel. number 555-3164 Date 10/5/-- Time 2:30 By pkb

Illustration 3-5

Telephone message form.

MESSAGES FROM OTHERS

Experience is a hard teacher because it gives the test first, the lessons afterwards.

—Unknown

Please hear what I am not saying.

—Kathleen Galvin and Cassandra Book

Date and time information helps the receiver know which call to return first. The person who called first should receive the first return call.

Sign your name or initials. The receiver of the message may want to ask questions about the call. Check your handwriting. Are the words readable? Are the numbers clear?

CHECKPOINT 3–4

YOUR GOAL: Get 3 or more main points of the message.

Complete the telephone message form below from Sam to Jane. Use the information from the sample telephone conversation between Sam and Caller on page 35.

Telephone Message

For ______________________ From ______________________

Would like you to call ☐ Left no message ☐

Returned your call ☐ Will call again ☐

Left the following message ______________________

____

____

Tel. number ______________ Date ______________ Time ______________ By ______________

☞ ***Check your work. Record your score.***

Message on Plain Paper

A scratch pad, the back of an envelope, or anything can be used for a message. However, your message still needs to be complete. Be sure to write clearly. Go through the checklist in Illustration 3-3 before putting down your pen or pencil. A message that you might write on plain paper is shown in Illustration 3-6.

Illustration 3-6

Message on plain paper.

8-23__ 9:00 a.m.

Jane
Please call Cristina Mendez at 555-8257. The phone of a neighbor. Sam

CHECKPOINT 3–5

YOUR GOAL: Get 3 or more main points of the message.

In the space provided, write a message for Eddie after the following conversation. Give yourself 1 point for each item of information you correctly provide.

REX: Hello!
CALLER: I want to talk to Eddie.
REX: Eddie isn't here right now.
CALLER: When will he be back?
REX: I am not sure. I would be glad to take a message and have him call you.
CALLER: Oh, I don't know what to do.
REX: This is his brother, Rex. Can I help you?
CALLER: No. I want him to come into work one hour early tomorrow. He is first on the list for overtime. I need an answer from him.
REX: I'll be happy to have him get in touch with you.
CALLER: OK, tell him to call Ralph, the line foreman, at 555-8167 extension 421 as soon as possible.

Check your work. Record your score.

MORE ABOUT FEEDBACK

The actions of the receiver of a message are called feedback.

As a listener you are expected to provide feedback. The actions of the receiver of a message are called **feedback**. Receiving information or listening is as important as speaking in the communication circle. If the speaker talks and the receiver doesn't listen, the circle is broken. If the listener doesn't take a correct message, the circle is broken.

Always play back the information you have received from the sender. Repeat what has been said. Ask for explanations if necessary. Wait for the sender to say you have the right information. Let's see how feedback works.

CONSUELA: Hello, warehouse. This is Consuela at the main plant.

HAROLD: This is Harold. How may I help you?

CONSUELA: We need a drive shaft sent with tomorrow's order. The number for the one we need is G-3472.

HAROLD: You said you need one drive shaft.

CONSUELA: Right. Thanks. Goodbye.

HAROLD: Wait a minute. Let me make sure I have this right. You want one drive shaft, number G-347 sent tomorrow.

CONSUELA: No, the number is G-3472.

HAROLD: Sorry, the drive shaft needed is G-3472.

CONSUELA: That's correct. Thank you.

HAROLD: Have a good day!

In this example, Harold made an extra effort to play back the information to Consuela. The extra effort paid off—Harold had written down the wrong drive shaft number. Try different phrases as you work at playing back messages. "Let me see if I have it straight . . . "; "Let me repeat that to make sure I have it right . . . "; "One more time . . . ."

CHECKPOINT 3–6

YOUR GOAL: Get 3 or more statements of feedback.

In the space provided, write the feedback you might give in a conversation. The first one is completed as an example. Give yourself 1 point for each correct response.

- What is your favorite color? Blue ______________________

1. You said you were not going to the plant. ______________________

____

2. Do you want to go to the community center? ______________________

____

3. How much does it cost to ride the bus to city center? ______________

____

4. I don't think the new tax on gasoline is fair. ____________________

____

5. I have three children. ______________________________

____

WHAT YOU HAVE LEARNED

- There are three basic methods of notetaking: writing an outline, writing a summary paragraph, or taking notes on a divided page.
- Messages must be taken accurately. When you are asked to pass on a message, don't trust your memory. Write it down.
- Feedback is an important part of communication and message taking. Play back all messages to the sender to be sure you took the message accurately.

PUTTING IT TOGETHER

ACTIVITY 3–1 **YOUR GOAL:** Get 3 or more of the main points of the message.

Outline the following information in the space provided. Give yourself 1 point for each main point of the summary you write.

STATUS SYMBOLS

A status symbol is something that people buy to impress others. The value of the object lies in what the object means to somebody else. Expensive cars have been traditional status symbols in America. They seem to suggest that the owners are used to wealth and luxury. A car may be bought to show that the owner has reached an important position in society.

Sometimes the symbol does not accurately reflect what is real. The owner of an expensive car may be having difficulty making the payments. He or she may be skimping on important items to put on a false front.

Think before you buy. Is this an item you need? Or, is this an item you are buying to impress others? Can you afford the product?

☞ ***Check your work. Record your score.***

ACTIVITY 3–2 **YOUR GOAL:** Get 2 or more of the main points of the message.

Read the following conversation between Li-ming and Angela. Write a summary paragraph for Angela in the space provided. Give yourself 1 point for each item of information you correctly provide.

LI-MING: There is a job opening at the restaurant where I work. The hours are 7:00 a.m. to 1:30 p.m. The work includes operating the cash register and seating customers.

ANGELA: What does it pay?

LI-MING: I am not sure.

ANGELA: What is the name of the restaurant?

LI-MING: The Oasis.

ANGELA: Where is it?

LI-MING: On the corner of 12th and Broadway.

ANGELA: Can I get there by bus?

LI-MING: Yeah, take the No. 1 Broadway bus and get off at 10th and Broadway. Walk two blocks north. You can't miss it. It's on the east side of the street.

Title: ______________________ Date: ______________________

Time: ______________________

____

____

____

____

____

☞ ***Check your work. Record your score.***

ACTIVITY 3–3 YOUR GOAL: Get 3 or more answers correct.

Complete the sentences in Column A with statements in Column B. Write the correct letter in the space provided. The first one is completed as an example. Give yourself 1 point for each correct answer.

Column A	Column B
• Notetaking helps you AA________	AA. remember the message.
1. The left side of divided-page notetaking ________	A. the main points.
2. Outline means writing down ______	B. date your notes.
3. It is important to ________	C. is for facts.
4. A summary paragraph is written when you ________	D. written on the right side of the divided page.
5. Questions are ________	E. cannot take notes while listening.

☞ ***Check your work. Record your score.***

ACTIVITY 3–4 YOUR GOAL: Complete 3 or more of the blanks correctly.

Fill in the message form provided after you have had the following conversation. Give yourself 1 point for each line correctly completed.

YOU: Robert's Grocery.
CALLER: Is Edith there? This is Dr. Craig's office.
YOU: No, this is her day off.
CALLER: Can I reach her at home?
YOU: I am not sure.
CALLER: Can you give me her number?
YOU: No, we do not give out employee numbers. May I take a message? She will be back tomorrow.
CALLER: Yes, ask her to call Dr. Craig's office. We need to reschedule her dental checkup.
YOU: The number please.
CALLER: 555-8168. Please ask her to call before noon.
YOU: OK, let me make sure I have everything. Call Dr. Craig's office before noon. The number is 555-8168.
CALLER: Correct. Thank you.
YOU: You are welcome. Goodbye.

Telephone Message

For ______________________ From ______________________

Would like you to call ☐ Left no message ☐

Returned your call ☐ Will call again ☐

Left the following message ______________________

____

____

Tel. number ____________ Date ____________ Time ____________ By ____________

☞ ***Check your work. Record your score.***

ACTIVITY 3–5 YOUR GOAL: Correctly underline 2 or more of the mistakes.

Underline the mistakes in the message taken following this conversation. Give yourself 1 point for each correctly underlined mistake.

IVAN: I'm calling to find out if I am eligible for Social Security benefits.
CLERK: Are you a senior citizen?
IVAN: No, I am disabled.
CLERK: Perhaps we can help you. Our benefits officers are in a meeting. May I have one of them call you?
IVAN: Yes. I am staying with my son Elijah Wather. His number is 555-7543.
CLERK: Your name please.
IVAN: Ivan Wather. I'll be here until 4:00 p.m.
CLERK: Someone will call you.
IVAN: Thanks, goodbye.

Message left on note pad.

Benefit Officer

Call Elijah Wather before 4:00 p.m.
He has questions about old-age benefits.
His number is 555-7534. He is staying with
someone named Ivan.

☞ ***Check your work. Record your score.***

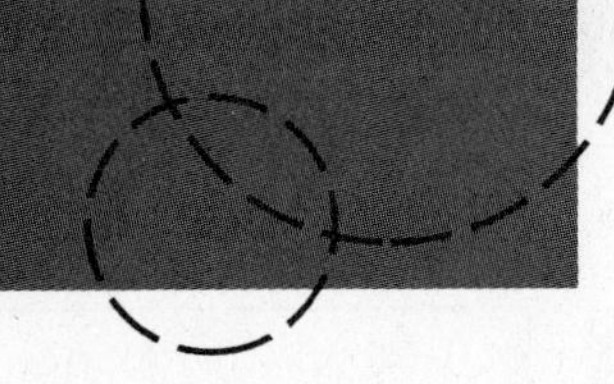

MAKING IT WORK

REVIEW I–1 YOUR GOAL: Get 18 or more correct.

Place a T in the space provided before true statements. Place an F in the space provided before false statements. The first one is completed as an example. Give yourself 1 point for each correct answer.

- T____ A listener or receiver accepts information.

1. _____ Messages give you information or direction, warn you of danger, alert you to the needs of others, or relax your mind.
2. _____ A sender receives ideas from a receiver.
3. _____ The sound of your voice helps others understand what you say.
4. _____ A message sent with the voice is called a nonverbal message.
5. _____ The nonverbal message is usually stronger than a verbal message.
6. _____ The actions of the receiver are called feedback.
7. _____ The circle of communication is complete when the receiver's feedback reaches the sender to end the process.
8. _____ The route that a message takes to get to the receiver is called the channel.
9. _____ More than one sense may be used to help send a message.
10. _____ Notetaking should be limited to the main ideas.
11. _____ Notetaking may not be appropriate in some situations.
12. _____ Notes should be reviewed as soon as possible.
13. _____ Do not sign your name or initials when you have taken a message for a friend.
14. _____ Noise is not a roadblock to listening.
15. _____ A poor attitude can keep you from listening well.
16. _____ If you get ahead of the speaker, use this time to review what the speaker has said.
17. _____ The selfish listener does not take responsibility for the conversation.
18. _____ The defensive listener likes to see things as others see them.
19. _____ An active listener thinks about what he or she is going to say when the speaker is finished.

20. ______ One responsibility of the listener is to separate the main thoughts from the opinions of the speaker.

☞ *Check your work. Record your score.*

REVIEW I–2 YOUR GOAL: Get 3 or more correct.

Match the terms in Column A with the statements in Column B. Write the correct letter in the space provided. The first one is completed as an example. Give yourself 1 point for each correct answer.

Column A	Column B
• __C__ Lazy listener	A. Process of sending and receiving information.
1. ______ Emotional listener	B. Item of communication which you are sending or receiving.
2. ______ Communication	C. Does not work hard to pay attention.
3. ______ Message	D. Is overwhelmed by feelings.
4. ______ Nonverbal message	E. Message without words.
5. ______ Channel	F. Route taken by a message.

☞ *Check your work. Record your score.*

REVIEW I–3 YOUR GOAL: Get 2 or more correct.

Fill in the parts of the circle of communication in the space provided. Give yourself 1 point for each correct answer.

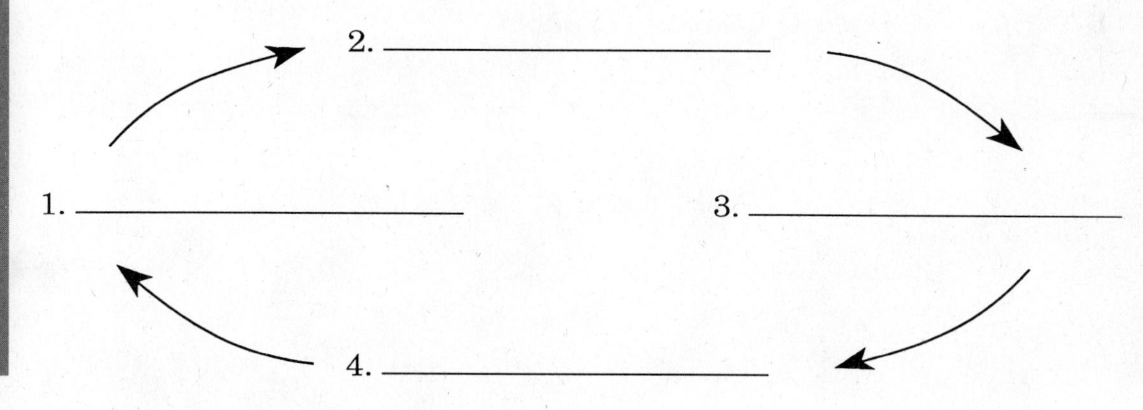

☞ *Check your work. Record your score.*

REVIEW I–4 YOUR GOAL: Get 7 or more correct.

In the space provided, write a message for Martha from Doug after the following conversation. You do not have a message form. Give yourself 1 point for each correct piece of information left in the message.

DOUG: Hello!

SUSIE: I want to speak with Martha.

DOUG: Martha isn't here right now.

SUSIE: When do you expect her?

DOUG: I don't know when to expect her. I would be happy to take a message for her.

SUSIE: OK. Please ask Martha to call Susie Michael at the Brownville Community Center. My number is 555-3827. Ask her to have her Social Security number handy when she calls.

DOUG: OK. I will leave a message for her.

SUSIE: Thanks for your help. I really need to speak with her today.

Check your work. Record your score.

PART TWO
LISTENING AND SPEAKING IN THE WORKPLACE

UNIT 4
LISTENING IN THE WORKPLACE

UNIT 5
SPEAKING IN THE WORKPLACE

UNIT 4
LISTENING IN THE WORKPLACE

WHAT YOU WILL LEARN

When you finish this unit you will be able to:

- Decide when to listen to supervisors, co-workers, and customers in the workplace.
- Distinguish between the formal and informal settings in which you listen in the workplace.

WORKPLACE LISTENING

Rewards of better listening on the job may mean more money. Workers must listen to suggestions in order to better do their jobs. To advance in a job, workers must have an awareness of what is going on in the business. This awareness can be gained by listening to supervisors, co-workers, and customers. Doing a job better because of your listening skills improves your chances of better pay.

The average worker spends almost half of his or her communication time in listening. Listening in the workplace is important as illustrated in Illustration 4-1.

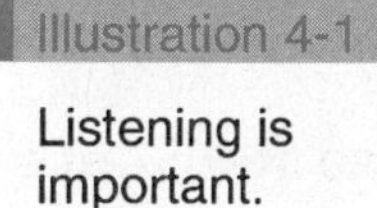

Illustration 4-1

Listening is important.

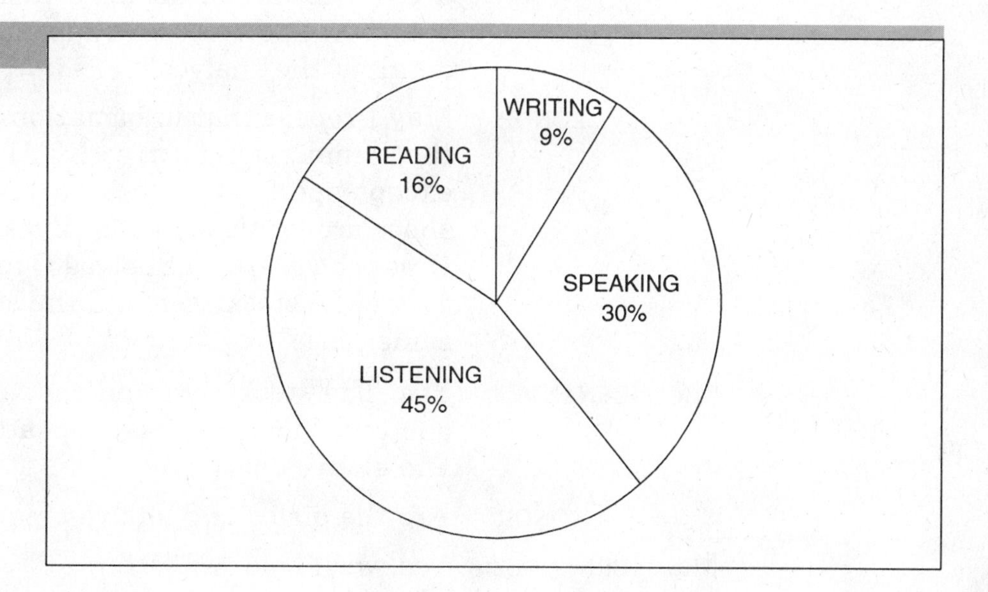

Listening to Supervisors

A supervisor is the person you report to.

A **supervisor** is anyone who directs and inspects your work. You report and answer to a supervisor. A supervisor directs the work of several people in a work area.

A supervisor may: (1) rate your ability to do a job, (2) determine your salary, (3) recommend you for a better paying job, (4) assist you in doing a job better, and (5) give workplace instructions. Each time you talk with your supervisor, make a effort to take notes. You can check your notes later to see if you are doing what was asked. Notetaking will also be a signal to your supervisor that you are serious about doing a good job. Ask your supervisor questions about any point you are not sure about. The more questions asked, the fewer mistakes made.

CHECKPOINT 4–1

YOUR GOAL: Get 4 or more answers correct.

Place an X beside each question that Leonor asked to understand her supervisor's directions. Give yourself 1 point for each correct answer.

MR. HERNANDEZ: Leonor, welcome to the Mid-City Shoe Store. Your job will be to restock shoes.

LEONOR: OK. Where are the stocking shelves?

MR. HERNANDEZ: In the stockroom behind the cash register.

MR. HERNANDEZ: Men's work shoes are in the storage room in Aisle 1 on Shelves A, B, and C. Men's dress shoes are in the same aisle on Shelves D and E. Sport shoes are located in Aisle 2 on all of the shelves.

LEONOR: May I repeat that information so I am sure that I understand correctly? All men's shoes except sport shoes are in Aisle 1. Work shoes are in Aisle 1 on Shelves A, B, and C. Dress shoes are on Shelves D and E in Aisle 1. Are the stockroom and the storeroom the same place?

MR. HERNANDEZ: Yes. The stockroom and the storeroom are one and the same. You repeated the aisles and shelves perfectly.

LEONOR: Are the aisles and shelves marked?

MR. HERNANDEZ: Yes, with bold red letters.

LEONOR: Do we sell women's shoes?

MR. HERNANDEZ: No. Mid-City Shoe Store offers quality shoes for men only.

LEONOR: Could we take a look at the stockroom?

☞ ***Check your work. Record your score.***

Listening to your supervisor will take many forms. You may be asked to order an item, call a customer, clean up a desk, or rearrange supplies. Whatever the request, listen carefully! Time and money are often lost because of poor listening skills.

Listening to Co-Workers

You will have many opportunities to listen to co-workers. They will provide you with information necessary to do your job. Co-workers will also share hints with you on how to do your job. They will also want you to listen to their work-related problems. Co-workers will want you to listen to their personal problems. This sounds like a lot of listening—it is! Your problem will be: How much do I listen to?

Your supervisor will want you to listen to shared information about how to do a job and how to help one another. However, most supervisors will prefer that you do not spend company time listening to problems and activities of others. So pay attention to what you are listening to. If you are listening to nonwork-related information, you may be putting yourself in an awkward position with your supervisor. Listening to co-workers is needed in order to become an accepted member of the work group. Personal listening should be saved for break and lunch times. These special times will provide you with the opportunity to listen to others as you choose.

Develop the habit of listening to all comments of your co-workers while on the job. Be ready to respond with quick, polite answers. If the co-workers are asking you to listen to nonwork-related information, you will want to be ready with some standard phrases. Try something like these remarks: "I would like to hear about your son's new job, but can it wait until break time?" "Please tell me about your bargain at lunch."

Listening to information related to how to do your job is acceptable at anytime. Remember these listening rules are correct whether or not your supervisor is present.

MESSAGES FROM OTHERS

Even if you're on the right track, you'll get run over if you just sit there.

—Will Rogers

Money is a terrible master but an excellent servant.

—P.T. Barnum

CHECKPOINT 4–2

YOUR GOAL: Get 5 or more answers correct.

Place an X in the space provided, showing when it would be appropriate to discuss the statement. The first one is completed as an example. Give yourself 1 point for each correct answer.

	Work Time	Break/ Lunch Time	
•	________	X	"I want to look for a new job."
1.	________	________	"Where are the cartons for this shipment?"
2.	________	________	"The top form goes with the order."
3.	________	________	"My son is getting married in June."
4.	________	________	"How is Tina ever going to pay for her car?"
5.	________	________	"The orange bin can be moved."
6.	________	________	"Where do we keep the postal supplies?"
7.	________	________	"I hope I can take a few days off this summer to visit my brother."

☞ ***Check your work. Record your score.***

Listening to Customers

A customer is a person who buys a product or service from your company.

Listening to the customers of your business is essential. A **customer** is one who buys a product or service from you or the business or organization you work for.

In most workplace settings, you will listen to customers every day in order to take care of their needs. In some businesses, customers will be called by other names: clients, patrons, taxpayers, or consumers. Whatever they are called, they deserve your ear and best attention.

Listen to every word of a customer. Don't block out any word. If you do, you may not correctly help the customer. For example:

CUSTOMER: I need a box of No. 2 pencils with eraser tips.

CLERK: Sure. (Goes to storage area and thinks, "A box of pencils with eraser tips.")

CLERK: Here you are. Will that be cash or charge?

CUSTOMER: I said No. 2 pencils; these are No. 3s.

CLERK: Sorry, I'll get a box of No. 2s.

The clerk didn't listen carefully to the full request of the customer. Repeating the request of the customer helps to remember it. The clerk blocked out the phrase, "No. 2 pencils." This action caused a delay in service to the customer, and cost the company extra time for the clerk. The worker should at all times listen actively to the wants and needs of the customer. This active listening includes watching the nonverbal communications of the customer. If a customer waves or gestures, you can assume that he or she needs help. Provide that help immediately. If the customer is handling the goods and looking them over carefully, this may be a signal that he or she wants help. Help immediately.

These clues can help the worker satisfy the wants or needs of the customer. Satisfying the customer will result in the customer returning to do business with the company. Customers are the most important part of any business. They deserve to be listened to by the worker.

Most workers who provide service of any kind depend on their listening skills to carry out their jobs. Every worker—dock worker, farm hand, shipping clerk, machine operator, barber—must listen to supervisors, co-workers, and customers.

WORKPLACE LISTENING OPPORTUNITIES

Group listening in the workplace will occur in formal and informal settings. Many of the listening rules are the same regardless of the setting. Let's take a look at some of the formal listening settings of the workplace.

Formal Settings

A formal setting may be a group or staff meeting. Receiving directions is a formal setting. Taking a message is also a formal setting. You may ask questions if you don't understand something. You may take notes.

Group/Staff Meetings

Meetings are called by your employer to explain new ways of doing things, new plans, an update on the condition of the company or reminders about company rules, as shown in Illustration 4-2. You may also see charts, graphs, and sales figures.

You should be prepared to take notes in this type of meeting. Listen carefully for the main points and jot them down for review later. Ask questions if you need to. Do not be afraid to ask questions. You were brought to the meeting to be informed.

Illustration 4-2

A formal opportunity to listen.

CHECKPOINT 4–3

YOUR GOAL: Write 3 or more reasons.

In the space provided, list reasons for calling a group meeting in a workplace. The first one is completed as an example. Give yourself 1 point for each reason you are able to list.

- **Explain new bus service to the plant.**

1. ______________________________
2. ______________________________
3. ______________________________
4. ______________________________
5. ______________________________

☞ ***Check your work. Record your score.***

Receiving Directions

You may be called to a special area to receive directions on a new way to complete a job. You may learn how to use a new

MESSAGES FROM OTHERS

If you really expect your "ship to come in," it would be wise to live near the sea.

—Unknown

We should all be concerned about the future because we will have to spend the rest of our lives there.

—Charles Kettering

machine. Or you may review safety rules. These meetings are certainly important listening opportunities. They are designed to help you. You must listen to be helped. Try these steps as you listen and follow directions: (1) Listen carefully, (2) ask questions, (3) try out the procedure, (4) ask for feedback, and (5) repeat. The example that follows gives directions on the safe use of a new saw within your plant.

SUPERVISOR: (Shows you how to use the new saw and talks about the importance of safety.)

YOU: Is the safety release marked with a red stripe or yellow stripe?

SUPERVISOR: It is marked by a red stripe.

YOU: May I try the saw while you watch?

SUPERVISOR: Sure go ahead.

YOU: (Try the procedure.) Was that correct?

SUPERVISOR: Looked good to me. You may want to press a little bit harder on the safety release when you finish your work.

YOU: Let me try it one more time.

SUPERVISOR: OK, I'll watch.

Can you identify the steps you took in following directions in the above example. A quick review of the steps can be found in Illustration 4-3.

Illustration 4-3

Steps to following instructions.

STEPS TO FOLLOWING INSTRUCTIONS

1. Listen carefully.
2. Ask questions.
3. Try out the procedure.
4. Ask for feedback.
5. Repeat the procedure.

Taking a Message

Messages are taken in formal listening settings. You know you are going to need to listen when you hear the phone ring in the workplace. When someone asks you face-to-face to take a message you listen. Review the checklist for taking a message. Just for practice fill in the telephone message form in Checkpoint 4–4.

CHECKPOINT 4–4

YOUR GOAL: Get 4 or more of the answers on the form.

Complete the telephone message form provided. Assume that you are Michi. Give yourself 1 point for each blank filled in correctly.

MICHI: Receiving Department. This is Michi.

DUANE: This is Duane with Greater Freight. I have a load of vegetables and I expect to be at your store in 25 minutes. Will you notify Pat Drake that I am on my way?

MICHI: Sure will. What purchase order number do you have for the delivery?

DUANE: Order No. 54839.

MICHI: OK, let me check. This is a message from Duane for Pat Drake. Greater Freight will be delivering vegetable Order No. 54839 in 25 minutes. I have 1:00 p.m. So, you'll be here about 1:25.

DUANE: Correct. Thanks.

Telephone Message

For ______________________ From ______________________

Would like you to call ☐ Left no message ☐

Returned your call ☐ Will call again ☐

Left the following message ______________________

____

____

Tel. number ____________ Date ____________ Time ____________ By ____________

☞ ***Check your work. Record your score.***

Informal Settings

Workplace information is not always gained in formal meetings. You will receive information from supervisors and co-workers in informal settings. The break room and hallways are informal settings. Meetings at the water cooler or at your workstation are informal meetings. Any number of other places within the workplace are informal settings. Be prepared to listen actively.

Co-Worker Information Sharing

Co-workers will usually share information with you at your workstation or on the job site as in Illustration 4-4. Listen carefully. When co-workers begin to share information not related to work, suggest that they save it for break or lunch. If the information shared is work-related, listen carefully and repeat the information to be sure you have it correct.

Illustration 4-4

Co-workers share work-related information.

Co-workers will also share information with you away from your workstation. You must determine whether the information being passed along is appropriate. You will find that sometimes listening is not appropriate. See the following examples: If the comments are disrespectful to your employer, you do not have to agree or disagree with the statements. If your co-worker shares information that you do not believe is your business, say "I would rather not hear that information." Smile and move on. If the information has an impact on your job, check out the accuracy of the information.

MESSAGES FROM OTHERS

Gossip runs faster over grapevines that are sour.

—Anonymous

It is easier to believe a lie that one has heard a thousand times than a fact no one ever heard before.

—Unknown

CHECKPOINT 4–5

YOUR GOAL: Get 3 or more of the answers correct.

Place an O in space provided before the sentence you would not listen to if shared by a co-worker at the water cooler. Place an X in the space provided before a statement you would check out. The first one is completed as an example. Give yourself 1 point for each correct answer.

___O___ • "I can't stand the way the new supervisor walks."

_______ 1. "Terry Long has been moved to our department."

_______ 2. "Did you hear that Tim's brother-in-law was picked up for burglary?"

_______ 3. "I heard that Mary Davis is going to be fired because she is always late."

_______ 4. "Our paychecks can be picked up at the pay window anytime after 3 p.m. today."

_______ 5. "I think the new plant manager is wearing a wig. Doesn't it look silly?"

☞ *Check your work. Record your score.*

Grapevine

The grapevine is an informal way of sending information from one worker to another by word of mouth.

Information can be gained in the workplace through what is called the **grapevine or gossip channels**. A grapevine is an informal way of passing information from one worker to another by word of mouth. Every workplace has a grapevine.

You should listen to grapevine information with care. Recognize that messages are often changed or added to as they pass from one person to another. Notice how a simple message in Illustration 4-5 changes as it passes from person to person.

Illustration 4-5 may be an extreme example. However, many messages become incorrect before reaching your listening ear. When you hear a message that is questionable, listen carefully. Repeat the message for accuracy. Then check with someone who would know the true story. Let grapevine gossip stop at your workstation.

Why does information change as it moves from person to person?

Sometimes people do not hear a part of the message.

Sometimes a word is added in place of a word that has been forgotten.

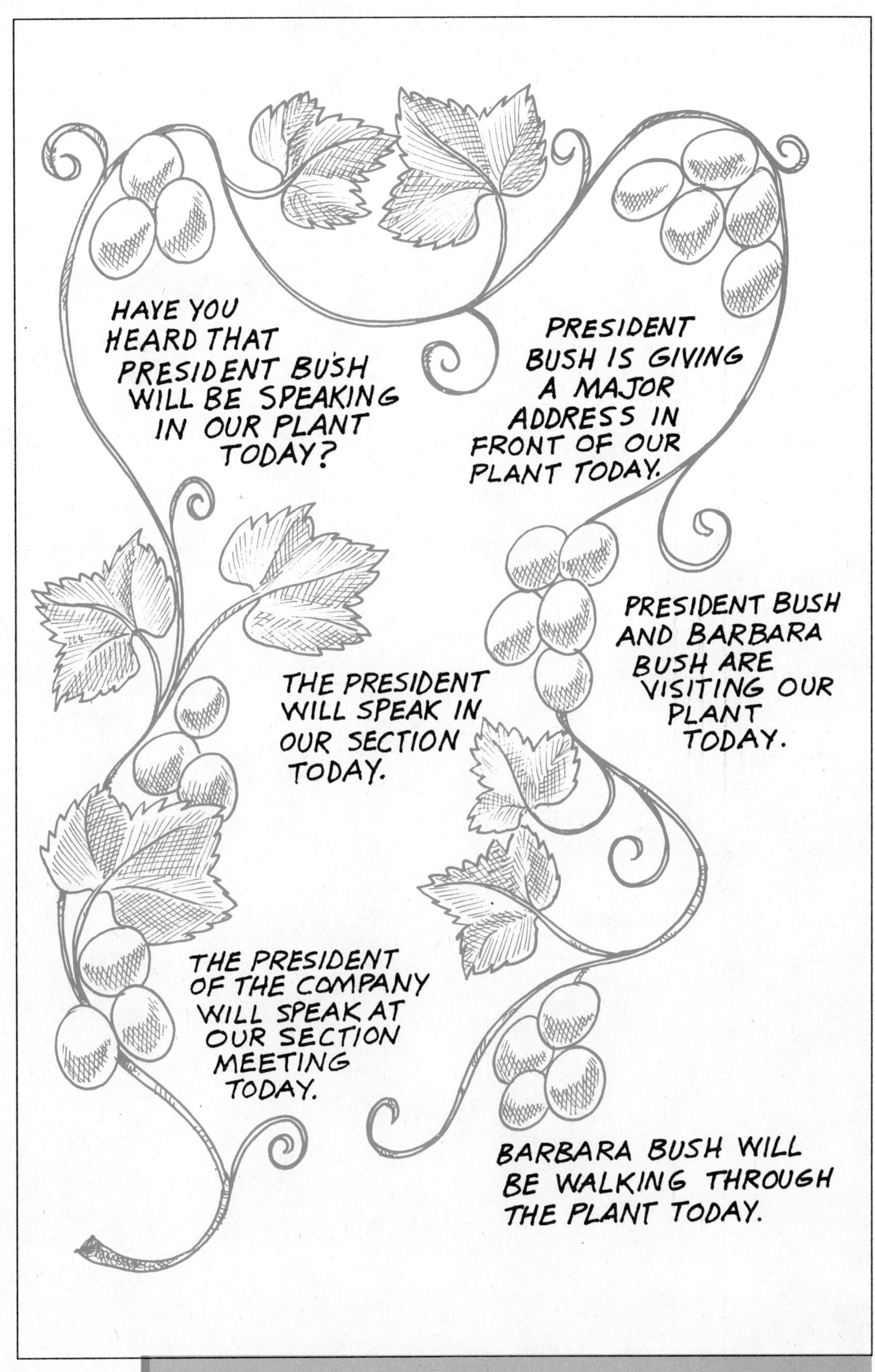

Illustration 4-5

Listen to the grapevine with care.

Sometimes a part of the message may have been forgotten.
Sometimes a person misinterprets what was said.

Grapevine information that is damaging to someone's character should not be listened to. Forget it. Don't even bother to check out the accuracy of the message. Avoid hurting a co-worker.

WHAT YOU HAVE LEARNED

- There are many individuals in the workplace whom you must listen to. These include supervisors, co-workers, and customers.
- You will listen to others in the workplace in formal and informal settings. Good listening is important in both settings. Grapevine information should be checked out before it is passed on to another worker.

PUTTING IT TOGETHER

ACTIVITY 4–1 YOUR GOAL: Get 1 or more questions.

Read the conversation. In the space provided, write questions that Juan should have asked. Give yourself 1 point for each question asked.

LOIS: Juan, I want to talk to you about the invoice we received for yesterday's shipment.

JUAN: OK.

LOIS: There are some mistakes here.

JUAN: Oh.

LOIS: I want you to make the corrections and notify the shipper.

____

____

____

____

____

____

____

☞ *Check your work. Record your score.*

ACTIVITY 4–2 YOUR GOAL: Get 3 or more answers correct.

Place an X in the space provided for those grapevine statements you would check for accuracy. Place an O for those statements you would just forget. The first one is completed as an example. Give yourself 1 point for each correct answer.

___O___ • "Mary Jane is dating the company manager."

_______ 1. "The bus routes from your area are being canceled."

_______ 2. "Anyone clocking in more than 3 minutes late will be fired."

_______ 3. "Todd looks like he stayed out all night."

_______ 4. "We can no longer drink coffee at our work stations."

_______ 5. "Tom is after Fumiko's job."

☞ *Check your work. Record your score.*

ACTIVITY 4–3 YOUR GOAL: Get 3 or more answers correct.

Place an X in the space provided for those topics which would be presented and discussed in a formal setting. If the topic would be presented and discussed in an informal setting, place an O in the space provided. The first one is completed as an example. Give yourself 1 point for each correct answer.

___X___ • The annual report of the company.

_______ 1. New company-wide procedure for filing insurance claims.

_______ 2. Demonstration of a new copy machine.

_______ 3. New fitness program for all workers.

_______ 4. Safety procedures for the welders.

_______ 5. Worker of the Year Award presentation.

☞ ***Check your work. Record your score.***

ACTIVITY 4–4 YOUR GOAL: Get 2 or more answers correct.

Write a response in the space provided to the topics which should not be discussed on company time. If the topic is appropriate for company time, write "OK" in the space provided. The first one is completed as an example. Give yourself 1 point for each correct answer.

- "Did you see Julio's new girlfriend pick him up last night?"

  No, I didn't. You can tell me about her at lunch.

1. "The new line supervisor asked me to keep an eye on Rod's work. What do you think she's after?"

   ____

2. "I found the greatest recipe for sauce to use in grilling chicken outside."

   ____

3. "Let me show you how to change the tape in that machine the easy way."

   ____

4. "I am looking for a good used VCR. Do you have any idea where I could get one?"

   ____

5. "Rachel wants to know if you and I will work overtime tonight."

   ____

☞ ***Check your work. Record your score.***

UNIT 5

SPEAKING IN THE WORKPLACE

WHAT YOU WILL LEARN

When you finish this unit, you will be able to:

- Prepare mentally to be a speaker in the workplace.
- Understand the situations that will require you to be a speaker in the workplace.
- Speak appropriately in special situations in the workplace.

PREPARATION FOR BEING A SPEAKER

You will be a speaker in the workplace. You will be a better speaker and communicator if you are prepared mentally.

How Do You See Yourself?

Take a look in the mirror. What do you see? You should see a person who has ideas and thoughts to share. You must recognize the value of your thoughts and ideas in order to communicate them. How many times have you been close to sharing an idea and then backed away? Then, a few moments later, someone else has the same idea, shares it, and is recognized for it. Now is the time for you to see yourself in your own mind as a worthy person. You are a worthy person with ideas and thoughts to express in the workplace.

How Do You Feel?

As you think about speaking and sharing with others, it is natural to feel a little uneasy. The best speakers, actors, and communicators get a few butterflies before speaking. The thought of speaking with others in the workplace should not be frightening. You were hired because you are a qualified worker. You were hired to share and communicate with others. Think positively of yourself, and others will think positive thoughts of you. Remember, you were chosen for the position.

Others can hear anger, sadness, happiness, and other emotions in your voice. In some cases, you may want to wait until you have control of your emotions. Remember to breathe to

Illustration 5-1

How do you see yourself?

keep oxygen going to your brain. You can think better when you breathe. You gain control of your emotions when you breathe.

How Do You Sound?

Listen to the sound of your voice. You may have a very soft voice. Perhaps your voice is difficult to hear. You will want to speak up. Make an extra effort to be sure that others hear what you have to say.

You may have a booming voice. Your voice may be too loud and bother others within the work area. You will need to work at toning down your voice. Speak more softly, but be sure to speak clearly.

You will want to appear skillful, competent, and interesting as you speak on the job. You can do this by feeling good about yourself and following the points in Illustration 5-2.

Illustration 5-2

Points to remember when speaking on the job.

POINTS TO REMEMBER WHEN SPEAKING ON THE JOB

1. Don't try to impress others.
2. Be yourself.
3. Use your own words as you ask questions or provide input.
4. Think about what you are saying.
5. Control your emotions—breathe.
6. Speak clearly and not to softly or loudly.

CHECKPOINT 5–1

YOUR GOAL: Get 3 or more answers correct.

In the space provided, complete the following statements about the points to remember when speaking on the job. The first one is completed as an example. Give yourself 1 point for each correct answer.

- Don't try to impress others.

1. ______________ yourself.
2. Use your own words as you ask questions or ______________ input.
3. Think about what you are ______________.
4. ______________ your emotions—breathe.
5. Speak ______________ and not too softly or too loudly.

☞ ***Check your work. Record your score.***

SPEAKING SITUATIONS ON THE JOB

You developed your speaking skills as you grew from childhood. You will also develop speaking skills in communicating with others as you grow on the job. You will be asked to share information and ideas, contact others, help solve problems, and influence others while you are on the job. Each speaking situation requires a review of Illustration 5-2.

Sharing and Providing Information

A major part of your speaking on the job will be sharing with and providing information to others. The basic rules for sharing information with co-workers, customers, and supervisors are the same. Let's take a look at the rules:

1. *Be polite.* Show an interest in providing the information that is being requested. Your words and the tone of your voice must be polite. Be eager and willing to share information.

   RAMON: Jason, can I ask you a question?
   JASON: Sure, I'll try to help.

2. *Be sure that you understand what is being asked.* Restate the information you think is being requested. Use your own words to rephrase the question.

RAMON: Jason, will you tell me how to find the paper we use for covers on the booklets sent to the Wong Corporation?

JASON: Sure, I think I can help. You want to know how to find the paper we use for covers on booklets we produce for the Wong Corporation.

RAMON: That's right.

3. *Share what you know.* Be specific in providing information. Provide all the information you know. If printed information, a sketch, or some type of drawing would be helpful in sharing information, *use it.*

JASON: Look in the file drawer labeled paper stock. Pull the file marked "Wong Corporation." You will find the stock number of the paper used on booklets for Wong. Susie, the stockroom clerk, will find the paper for you if you provide her with the number.

RAMON: Thanks for your help.

4. *Refer to another person if you don't know.* If you don't know or are not sure of the information being asked, try to help by referring the person to someone else. You may need to assist her or him in finding others who can provide the information needed.

5. *Ask if the information you have shared is adequate.* To complete the circle of communication, be sure to check your feedback with the person you are providing information for.

JASON: Does that take care of what you needed to know?

RAMON: Sure does. Thanks again.

6. *Don't use the sharing of information as an opportunity to start or continue a nonwork-related conversation.* You should provide the information requested in a willing manner and go on with your work.

JASON: By the way, do you know of any sales on bowling balls? I sure would like to pick up a new ball before the fall season starts.

7. *Show that you are willing to provide help and share information in the future.* Your willingness to help will encourage others to continue to ask for help. You will build goodwill with co-workers, customers, and supervisors.

JASON: Always glad to help. Let me know if you find the paper.

MESSAGES FROM OTHERS

Confidence does more to make conversation than wit.

—LaRochefoucauld

A good conversationalist is not one who remembers what was said, but says what someone wants to remember.

—John Mason Brown

CHECKPOINT 5–2

YOUR GOAL: Get 6 or more answers correct.

Place a T in the space provided if the statement is true. Place an F in the space provided if the statement is false. The first one is completed as an example. Give yourself 1 point for each correct answer.

___F___ • Do not refer questions to another person.

________ 1. Do not use an illustration to answer a question.

________ 2. Politeness in answering questions is important.

________ 3. Restate a question if you are not sure what was asked.

________ 4. Use your own words when you rephrase questions.

________ 5. A major part of speaking on the job will be sharing information with others.

________ 6. Use the sharing of information as a way to start a nonwork-related conversation.

________ 7. Avoid referring questions to others.

________ 8. Check to make sure the information shared is adequate.

☞ ***Check your work. Record your score.***

Requesting Information

You will often need to seek information from others. You will need to ask questions of your co-workers, supervisors, and perhaps even customers. Before you ask a co-worker or a supervisor for information, be sure that you have tried to find the answer first. You don't want to take up the time of others unless it is necessary.

You may need to request information from customers in order to better understand their needs. For example:

YOU: Marshall's Hardware. May I help you?

CUSTOMER: Yes, I would like some burner covers for my range.

YOU: What brand of range do you own?

CUSTOMER: I have a Top-Point.

YOU: Is your Top-Point fueled by gas or electricity?

CUSTOMER: It is a gas range.

YOU: Do you have a particular color in mind? The covers come in harvest gold, almond, and black.

Your questions should help the customer clarify his or her order. These questions will help the customers get what they want.

Requesting Action

Sometimes you may need to ask a co-worker to do something for you. State your questions or requests for action so that they are easily understood. State your requests in simple terms. Most people like straight-forward questions. A good way to state your request is using the AEA request formula explained in Illustration 5-3.

Illustration 5-3

Request formula.

HOW TO MAKE A ROUTINE REQUEST

A = Ask for the information or action to be taken.
E = Explain your need in brief terms.
A = Appreciate by thanking your supervisor or co-worker for the help and cooperation.

For example, see how Vincente asks Carol to trade lunch hours, provides a brief explanation, and then expresses appreciation.

VINCENTE: Carol, I would like to trade lunch hours with you on Thursday. I need to go to lunch from 12:30 to 1:30 p.m. My scheduled hour is 11:30 a.m. to 12:30 p.m. I want to see my son in a school program. Are you willing to trade with me?

The feedback from your request will let you know if the request was understood.

CAROL: Vincente, I will be glad to trade lunch hours with you on Thursday. Please remind me on Wednesday of our agreement.

VINCENTE: Thanks. I appreciate your willingness to help me. I'll talk with you on Wednesday.

Persuading Others

Persuasion is attempting to get others to adopt or agree with an idea that you have.

Persuasuion is attempting to get others to adopt or agree with an idea that you have. On-the-job speaking will include getting others to agree with you.

You will want and need at various times to persuade customers, co-workers, and supervisors. Part of your job may be to persuade customers to use a product or service of your employer.

You will need to get the attention of the customer, co-worker, or supervisor. You must show your audience why your idea, product, or service is the best. Two ways to persuade others are discussed. One approach is to ask a question:

Did you know one glass of our juice provides 90 percent of the vitamins your baby needs?
Would you like to help the people of your community?

The questions are positive and bring to mind happy thoughts. These questions put your listener in the mood to hear what you have to say. The question approach is very good for persuading customers.

LOU: Oki, do you want what is best for your baby?
OKI: Of course!

JOHN: Would you like to save money on gas?
JUDY: Sure, how can I do that?

Another approach is to tell a story. Everyone likes to hear a good story. The story must relate closely to the message you want your customer, co-worker, or supervisor to hear. Keep your story brief. The story doesn't have to be funny. The story probably will be about something you have experienced in your life. An example of a story to persuade follows:

Let me tell you about my friend Elmer. Elmer thought he didn't need to join in the fun of a block party. He chose to just sit on his porch and watch. One of the kids threw him a ball. Of course, he wanted to throw it back. Before Elmer knew it, he was joining in the fun. I know

> **MESSAGES FROM OTHERS**
>
> Watch your speech. A person's command of the language is more important. Next to kissing, it's the most exciting form of communication mankind has evolved.
>
> —Oren Arnold

you would enjoy bowling with us after work. Do you want to give it a try?

Perhaps a story like this one would help you to get a co-worker to join the department bowling team. Other stories could help get a supervisor to listen to an idea of yours or persuade a customer to try a new product or service.

CHECKPOINT 5–3

YOUR GOAL: Get 3 or more answers correct.

Complete the following statements with the words at the end of the statements. Write the words in the space provided. The first one is completed as an example. Give yourself 1 point for each correct answer.

- Before you ask a co-worker or supervisor for information, be sure you have tried to find the answer first.

1. Your ______________ can help the customer clarify his or her order.
2. State your ____________________ so that they are easily understood.
3. The AEA formula means ask, _________________, and appreciate.
4. Persuasion is the ______________ to get others to agree with you.
5. To persuade a customer, you may ask a question or tell the customer a______________ .

Attempt, Explain, First, Questions, Requests, Story.

☞ ***Check your work. Record your score.***

SPECIAL OPPORTUNITIES FOR SPEAKING ON THE JOB

You will speak in many situations on the job. You begin a job by speaking at a job interview. You will respond to questions.

You will respond to comments made by your supervisor when your work is reviewed or evaluated.

Employment Interview

What you say at the employment interview may determine whether or not you get the job. You should prepare for the interview by thinking about some of the questions you may be asked. Be prepared to talk about your previous jobs. You will talk about your background and experiences that are related to the type of job you are applying for. Some questions you can expect might include:

"What type of work have you been doing?"

"Do you enjoy working outdoors or indoors?"

"Will you tell me a little bit about yourself?"

"Why do you feel you are qualified for this position?"

Your voice should be clear and loud enough for the interviewer to hear your answers. Look at the interviewer as you answer questions, as shown in Illustration 5-4. If you do not understand a question, ask that the question be repeated or restated. For example:

INTERVIEWER: Have you ever worked in low coal?

AUDREY: I don't know what you mean by low coal.

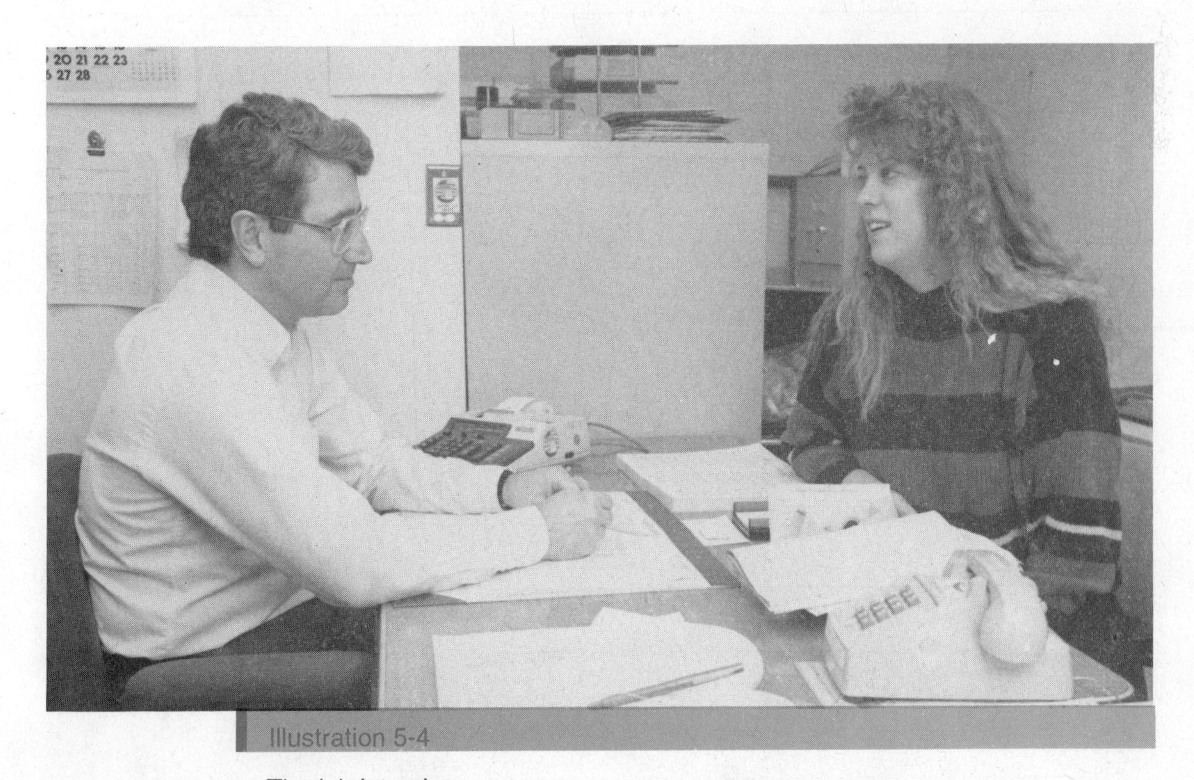

Illustration 5-4

The job interview.

Your answers should be honest and straight-forward. It is all right to take a few seconds to put your thoughts together before answering a question. Avoid answering with only "yes" or "no." Try to state at least one complete thought as you respond to a question. For example: "Have you ever worked in a forestry operation?" If your answer is "no," you might say: "I haven't had the opportunity to work in forestry, but I enjoy the outdoors." If your answer is "yes," give a little information. For example: "Yes, I worked in the forests of Wisconsin as a firefighter."

CHECKPOINT 5–4

YOUR GOAL: Get 3 or more questions answered.

Write your answers to the job interview questions in the space provided. The job you are applying for is a position as a trainee with the forestry service. Give yourself 1 point for each answer you can provide.

- Why did you leave your last job?

  My job was cut because of a slowdown in demand for the products we were building.

1. What jobs have you held in the last two years?

   ____

   ____

   ____

2. Do you enjoy working outdoors?

   ____

   ____

   ____

3. When could you begin working?

   ____

   ____

   ____

4. Why do you think you would be successful in this position?

   ____

____

____

5. Are you willing to travel?

____

____

____

☞ ***Check your work. Record your score.***

You will want to have questions ready for the interviewer. Plan ahead. Write your questions on a small piece of paper or a card and take it with you. Some sample questions might be:

"What hours would I be working?"

"Is there a fringe-benefit package?"

"Will you tell me a little more about the job than is described in the ad?"

"Is this a permanent position?"

You will be expected to ask questions. Good questions will help the interviewer know that you are interested in the job.

Work Reviews

Your work will be reviewed or evaluated by a supervisor. In most positions, work reviews occur at least before the end of a 90-day trial period. Your work may be reviewed again after the first six months and annually thereafter. This review should let you know how you are doing on the job. Do not look at this review as a scary or threatening situation. Look at the review as an opportunity to improve on the job. Be prepared for the review by thinking about questions you have about your work. You may want to write these questions down and take them to the review with you. You should look at the reviewer and show interest in what is being discussed. Let the reviewer know that you are listening, by responding with a nod of the head or a brief comment. For example:

REVIEWER: Megan, I am pleased with the work you are doing as a production worker.

MEGAN: Thank you. I enjoy my work.

The review that goes well for you is easy to respond to. You listen, you ask your questions, and then you thank the reviewer for his or her time and suggestions. However, if the review does not go well for you and you receive many suggestions--or even a warning that you will be fired--you will need to follow a different procedure. The steps in Illustration 5-5 will help you know what to do if the review is not going well for you.

Illustration 5-5

How to handle a difficult work review.

HOW TO HANDLE A DIFFICULT WORK REVIEW

Step 1: Listen carefully. Give nonverbal responses to the reviewer to indicate that you are listening.

Step 2: Ask questions to clarify the concerns of the reviewer.

Step 3: If there are some differences of opinion or points of confusion about your work, state your side of the story in honest, straight-forward terms. (Be careful to keep an even tone of voice.)

Step 4: Indicate that you will work to improve. Ask for help in the future.

Step 5: Thank the reviewer for his or her time.

CHECKPOINT 5–5

YOUR GOAL: Get 3 or more answers correct.

Unscramble the letters to show the steps of handling a difficult work review. Write your answers in the space provided. Give yourself 1 point for each correct answer.

- ksA rof pleh ni eth retufu.

  Ask for help in the future.

1. netsiL yllfuacre.

   ____

2. skA ionstques ot yfiralc teh ccsnreno.

   ____

   ____

3. tateS ouyr edis fo teh yrots.

   ____

4. etacidnL ttah uoy llwi krow ot evorpmi.

____

____

5. nkahT het eewriver ofr sih ro reh emit.

____

____

☞ *Check your work. Record your score.*

WHAT YOU HAVE LEARNED

- The importance of preparing mentally to speak in the workplace, and points to remember when speaking on the job.
- Your role in sharing and providing information, requesting information, requesting action, and persuading others.
- Tips on speaking in a job interview and in a work review.

PUTTING IT TOGETHER

ACTIVITY 5–1 **YOUR GOAL:** Get 3 or more answers correct.

Place an X in the space provided if the response to the situation is appropriate. Place a O in the space provided if the response is not appropriate. Then briefly explain why you placed an X or an O. Give yourself 1 point for each correct answer.

- Situation: Nicolas has asked you a question about working overtime. You do not know the answer.

  __X__ I'm sorry, Nicolas. I don't know the answer. I am sure that Elsie in the Personnel Department can help you.

  Why? **Answer was direct. Nicolas was directed to another person for help.**

1. Situation: Meredith has been working about 10 minutes trying to get a paper jam out of the copy machine. She asks for your help.

   ________ Sure. I'll try to help you. Let's get out the manual and see if paper jams are explained.

   Why? ____

   ____

2. Situation: Ileana is trying to deliver a package for her employer. The street signs are confusing. She asks for your help.

   ________ The street you are looking for is on the other side of the railroad tracks. Go to the tracks and turn left at the first traffic light. Go south about seven or eight blocks. You will see the street sign on the east side of the road.

   Why? ____

   ____

3. Situation: Tyron says to you, "Will you please show me how to get this forklift out of gear?"

   ________ Sure. All you need to do is hold down the lever marked with a red G. Can you help Joe and me move this weekend?

   Why? ____

   ____

☞ *Check your work. Record your score.*

ACTIVITY 5–2 YOUR GOAL: Get 2 or more answers correct.

In the space provided, write what you would say to a customer or co-worker to try and persuade him or her to use the product or to agree with you. The first one is completed as an example. Give yourself 1 point for each correct answer.

- You are selling soft drinks in the stands at a major league football game.

  Did you know that Joe Montana drinks one of these at halftime?

1. You are trying to get a customer to sample the ice cream you are selling.

   ____

   ____

   ____

2. You want Hedy, your co-worker, to trade hours work with you, and she doesn't particularly want to.

   ____

   ____

   ____

3. You want a co-worker to try to use an easy method of bundling papers for recycling. The co-worker doesn't like change.

   ____

   ____

   ____

4. A customer prefers to use a brand of soap he or she has been using for years. You want to convince him or her that Slide Soap is better.

   ____

   ____

   ____

☞ ***Check your work. Record your score.***

ACTIVITY 5–3 YOUR GOAL: Get 2 or more answers correct.

In the space provided, write a question that you would expect at a job interview. Then write in the space provided the answer that you would give to the question. Give yourself 1 point for each correct answer.

1. Question: ______________________________

   ____

2. Answer: ______________________________

   ____

In the space provided, write a question you would expect to ask at a job review session.

3. ______________________________

   ____

   ____

   ____

☞ ***Check your work. Record your score.***

MAKING IT WORK

REVIEW II–1 YOUR GOAL: Get 3 or more correct.

List five topics in the space provided which would not be appropriate to discuss with a co-worker during work hours. The first one is completed as an example. Give yourself 1 point for each topic you can list.

- **A family discussion.**

1. ______________________________
2. ______________________________
3. ______________________________
4. ______________________________
5. ______________________________

☞ ***Check your work. Record your score.***

REVIEW II–2 YOUR GOAL: Get 3 or more correct.

In the space provided, list the steps to following instructions. The first step is listed for you. Give yourself 1 point for each correct answer.

1. **Listen carefully.**
2. ______________________________
3. ______________________________
4. ______________________________
5. ______________________________

☞ ***Check your work. Record your score.***

REVIEW II–3 YOUR GOAL: Get 8 or more correct.

Place a T in the space provided if the statement is true. Place an F in the space provided if the statement is false. The first one is completed as an example. Give yourself 1 point for each correct answer.

__T__ • Messages are taken in formal listening settings.

______ 1. Workplace information is not always gained in formal meetings.

______ 2. If co-workers share information that does not relate to work, listen carefully while at the workstation.

_______ 3. Avoid asking questions in staff meetings.

_______ 4. A customer is a person who buys a product or service from you or the business organization you work for.

_______ 5. Personal listening should be saved for break and lunch times.

_______ 6. Try to impress others while speaking on the job.

_______ 7. A booming voice may be difficult to listen to.

_______ 8. Restate information you think is being requested.

_______ 9. Avoid using illustrations, sketches, or other printed information when sharing information.

_______ 10. Use your own words when you rephrase questions.

☞ ***Check your work. Record your score.***

REVIEW II–4 YOUR GOAL: Get 4 points.

Complete the following activities in the space provided. Give yourself 2 points for each completed answer.

1. Write what you would say to ask a co-worker to cover the telephone for you while you assist another co-worker with a new procedure. Use the AEA formula.

____

____

____

____

____

____

2. Write a short story that you could use to persuade a customer to try a new car wax that your business is promoting.

____

____

____

____

3. In the space provided, write an answer to the following job interview questions. You are applying for a job as a caretaker in a small-town animal shelter.

   a. What experience have you had with caring for animals other than dogs and cats?

   ____

   ____

   ____

   ____

   ____

   b. What types of questions would you ask a patron who is considering adopting a pet?

   ____

   ____

   ____

   ____

   ____

☞ ***Check your work. Record your score.***

PART THREE
PERSONAL LISTENING AND SPEAKING SKILLS

UNIT 6
EVERYDAY LISTENING AND SPEAKING

UNIT 7
POLISHING YOUR SPEAKING SKILLS

UNIT 8
YOUR CHANCE TO SPEAK OUT

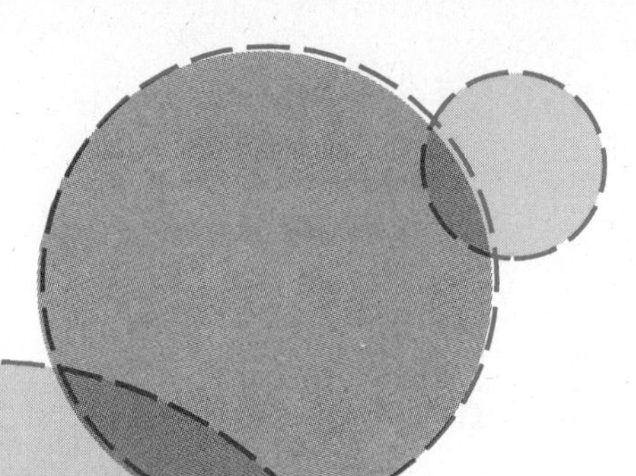

UNIT 6
EVERYDAY LISTENING AND SPEAKING

WHAT YOU WILL LEARN

When you finish this unit you will be able to:

- Understand your role as a listener and speaker in everyday life.
- Be a comfortable conversationalist in many situations.

PERSONAL LISTENING AND SPEAKING

A human being is one who is able to work, love, play, and communicate with others.

Getting to know people is essential to being a **human being.** A human being is one who is able to work, love, play, and communicate with others. A human being can contribute something to living better. Human behavior depends upon knowing people. The way you get to know others is by listening and speaking with them.

You as a Listener

Everyone knows that some people are much more fun to talk to than others. Have you found that there are some friends to whom you just feel like talking? Do you know others around whom you feel that you have nothing to say? Can you explain the difference?

Don't you enjoy talking to the person who acts truly interested in what you have to say and shows it? To make yourself a good conversationalist, you must be a good listener. This means you must show that you are interested in what is being said. You cannot just sit back and be quiet. On the other hand, good listeners do not constantly interrupt or wait breathlessly for a pause so that they can say what is on their minds. Illustration 6-1 gives you some cues for how to let others know you are a good listener.

Courteous listening brings out the best in those to whom you are listening. This is true whether you are in an individual or group conversation or in an audience.

Illustration 6-1

Guides for listening in conversation.

GUIDES FOR LISTENING IN CONVERSATION

1. Look at the speaker with an interested expression.
2. Do not fiddle with keys, a pencil or other objects.
3. Indicate interest by nodding, frowning, or smiling at the right time so that the speaker knows that you are listening.

CHECKPOINT 6–1

YOUR GOAL: Get 1 or more answers correct.

Think about two people you most like to talk to. In the space provided, list two reasons you like to talk with them. Give yourself 1 point for each reason listed.

1. ______________________________

____

2. ______________________________

____

☞ ***Check your work. Record your score.***

Your Listening Body Language

There are several body movements that you will want to avoid as a listener. You must learn to have an open face and an open body. An open face means a face willing to listen and accept new ideas. A face with a frown is not an open face. A pleasant, interested look will indicate you are open to hear new ideas and thoughts. Let your listener know you are listening by looking at him or her, lifting your eyebrows, and nodding your head. Illustration 6-1 reminds you to look at the speaking person. If looking into someone's eyes causes you to be uncomfortable, look at another part of his or her face. Try looking at the nose, the mouth, or the eyebrows. Eventually, you will train yourself to look into the eyes of others.

An open body stance is also important. Do not stand or sit with your arms crossed over the chest. This gives the speaker the feeling that you are not agreeing or not accepting what is being said. Keep your body open. Hands crossed in front of your body also indicate a closed look. Keep your hands at your side. Or, perhaps one hand in a pocket. Compare two examples of listening body language shown in Illustration 6-2.

Illustration 6-2

Closed body vs. open body.

You as a Speaker

You will want to communicate thoughts of interest as you speak. The topics of your conversation are important. You will want to speak about topics that interest you and others. You will want to speak in a lively manner.

Starting a conversation with a good friend is easy. It almost starts itself. Carrying on a conversation with someone you don't know well may not be so easy. Finding a topic of interest to you both may present a problem, but there are ways to solve it. Mention or ask a question about something that has happened at work or in school. A current movie, a television program, or a magazine or newspaper headline you have noticed are good topics. The chances of your favorite football or basketball team winning the next game may start a conversation.

If you fail to get a conversation going with the first few topics you introduce, keep trying. Sooner or later you will hit upon something that will get the other person talking. Most people want to be friendly, but some of them are shy. Perhaps you are shy yourself. If so, you know how much you appreciate someone who can bring you into the conversation.

A good technique to use in starting a conversation is to ask a question. The question will encourage a response from the other person. His or her answer will let you know if the topic you are trying out is a good one. For example:

YOU: Did you hear the final score of the Green Bay, Cincinnati Bengals football game?

MYRA: Yes, it was 42 to 35. Cincinnati won. I really enjoyed the game.

MESSAGES FROM OTHERS

It is the I behind the eye that sees.

—Anonymous

Knowledge is of two kinds: we know a subject ourselves, or we know where we can find information about it.

—Samuel Johnson

Myra's response to you would indicate that she likes to talk about football. You are off to a good start.

YOU: Did you hear the final score of the Green Bay, Cincinnati Bengals football game?

MYRA: No. I don't follow football.

Oops! You know football is the wrong topic to begin a conversation with Myra. Try again.

Speaking Body Language

Your body can take away the meaning of your spoken message. Don't allow your movements and gestures to detract from what you are saying. Avoid the following meaningless or repeated gestures: scratching your head, pacing back and forth, rocking from foot to foot, fussing with your clothes, or twisting your hands.

Building Conversation Skills

Conversations should take place naturally, helped by the thoughtfulness and interest of those who take part. Illustration 6-3 offers some guides that may help build your conversational skills.

Illustration 6-3

Guides for participating in a conversation.

GUIDES FOR PARTICIPATING IN A CONVERSATION

1. Be friendly.
2. Choose interesting subjects to talk about.
3. Let your manner be easy and informal.
4. Contribute your ideas and encourage others to contribute theirs.
5. Disagree pleasantly if you disagree. Differences of opinion often put energy into the conversation.
6. Be polite and wait your turn to talk.
7. Allow your sense of humor to show in conversation.

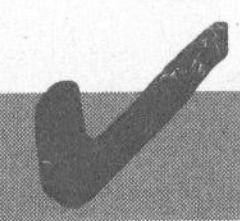

CHECKPOINT 6–2

YOUR GOAL: Get 2 or more answers correct.

List four topics you feel comfortable talking about. Follow the topic with an opening sentence in the space provided that you think would help start a conversation. The first one is completed as an example. Give yourself 1 point for each topic followed by an opening sentence.

- Topic: **Weather**

  Opening sentence: **Have you heard the weather forecast for the weekend?**

1. Topic: ______________________________

   Opening sentence: ______________________________

   ____

   ____

2. Topic: ______________________________

   Opening sentence: ______________________________

   ____

   ____

3. Topic: ______________________________

   Opening sentence: ______________________________

   ____

   ____

4. Topic: ______________________________

   Opening sentence: ______________________________

   ____

   ____

☞ ***Check your work. Record your score.***

PERSONAL CONVERSATIONAL EXPERIENCES

Each day of your life you will have personal conversation experiences. Perhaps you will need to introduce one person to another. You may help others begin a conversation or tell a story. You may need to set an appointment or just make one-to-one small talk. You can be very successful in each of these experiences with a little practice.

Making Introductions

Introduce people to each other as soon as possible. People feel awkward and uncomfortable if introductions are not made very quickly. Say the name of an older person first when you introduce a younger person to an older person. Review these examples:

YOU: Mr. Chiang, this is Lydia Thone, who has just moved into our building. Lydia, I want you to met Mr. Chiang.

YOU: Mother, I'd like you to meet Dave Hogan. Dave Hogan, this is my mother, ____________ .

Illustration 6-4

Making an introduction.

MESSAGES FROM OTHERS

The only way to have a friend is to be one.

—Emerson

Our todays and yesterdays are the blocks with which we build.

—Anonymous

The tongue is but three inches long, yet it can kill a man six feet high.

—Japanese Proverb

Avoid the trite expressions like "Meet Dave Hogan" or "Shake hands with Dave" or "Say hello to Dave." It is better to say simply, "This is Dave Hogan" or "I'd like you to meet Dave Hogan."

Do not hesitate to introduce yourself if you are a stranger in a group. You can simply say, "Hi, I am John Doe." The others will then automatically introduce themselves. If you meet someone you don't know, say "Hello, I am John Doe, and what is your name?"

Be sure you acknowledge an introduction. Say, "How do you do, Mr. Smith?" Or, you may want to add, "I am very glad to meet you." Avoid the worn-out expression, "Pleased to meet you."

A young person who is seated should stand if one of the persons being introduced is much older. You do not have to stand if you are introduced to someone your own age who is standing. It is courteous to shake hands with anyone who extends his or her hand to you in an introduction. If you do shake hands, grip the other person's hand firmly. Limp handshakes are not appropriate in any situation.

When you introduce people, one of your responsibilities is to give them some fuel for conversation. Tell something about one or both of the people being introduced to help them begin a conversation. An **icebreaker** is a topic that helps to start a conversation.

An icebreaker is a topic that helps to start a conversation.

For example, in an introduction:

YOU: Joan, I'd like you to meet Yolanda Collins. This is Joan McDouglas, Yolanda. (Icebreaker) Yolanda has just moved here from New Jersey. I know you have relatives in New Jersey, Joan.

You have now set the stage for Joan and Yolanda to open a conversation. They know something they have in common to talk about. Whenever you are given the opportunity to introduce people, make it a habit to help them out by tossing in an icebreaker.

CHECKPOINT 6–3

YOUR GOAL: Get 1 or more introductions written.

Write out introductions for the following situations in the space provided. Give yourself 1 point for each introduction written.

1. You and a stranger walk into a party at about the same time. You know that you must introduce yourself. What are you going to say?

 ____

 ____

 ____

 ____

2. You introduce a senior citizen, Guy Ingles, to your young friend, Sharon Meyer. Sharon came from Guy's home town, Hunterville.

 ____

 ____

 ____

 ____

☞ ***Check your work. Record your score.***

Telling a Story

Sometimes a topic of conversation brings to mind a humorous or exciting story about an experience you have had. Don't be afraid to tell a story that will entertain someone or illustrate a point. Everyone enjoys listening to good stories. Keep in mind, stories do not have to be funny in order to be interesting and meaningful. Illustration 6-5 provides some helpful hints for telling a story.

Setting an Appointment

Appointments are a part of your daily life. You may have appointments with doctors, dentists, social service workers, and your children's teachers to name a few. You should schedule appointments to use your time and the time of others wisely. When you set an appointment, be sure that the time is free for you. Be sure the person you are setting the appointment with knows who you are. Be sure the person knows what the appointment is for. Ask if any special information should be

Illustration 6-5

Hints for story-telling.

HINTS FOR STORYTELLING

1. Connect the story with the subject of the conversation.
2. Begin your story with a quick, interesting sentence.
3. Avoid giving details which do not help to make a point or to set the mood of the story.
4. Use actual thoughts or dialogue to increase interest.
5. Build suspense, if the story allows.
6. Avoid expressions like "It was very funny" or "It was very exciting."
7. Avoid interrupting your story with uhs and ands.

brought to the appointment. Verify the date, place, and time of your appointment. The following example shows how an appointment should be scheduled:

MR. BELLA: Ms. Farlow, I am Carmen Bella's father. I would like to talk with you.

MS. FARLOW: Certainly, Mr. Bella.

MR. BELLA: Would 4:00 p.m. on Friday, October 16, be convenient for you?

MS. FARLOW: Yes, that would be fine.

MR. BELLA: I want you to better understand Carmen's hearing problem. Do you want me to bring the information her doctor has supplied?

MS. FARLOW: Yes, if you think it would be helpful.

MR. BELLA: Yes, I do. I'll report to the school office on Friday, October 16, at 4:00 p.m.

MS. FARLOW: I'll look forward to meeting you.

One-to-One Conversations

You will speak on a daily basis to friends, neighbors, and family members. These conversations are important. Make sure that you have eye contact with the person you are speaking to. Do not stand too close to the person you are speaking with. If you stand too close, you may make the other person uncomfortable. The standard rule for distance when speaking to another person is about 18 inches. Watch for nonverbal clues of your listener. Does he or she understand what you are saying? Are you getting your ideas across? Does the listener have a question?

CHECKPOINT 6–4

YOUR GOAL: Get 3 or more answers correct.

Place a T in the space provided if the statement is true. Place an F in the space provided if the statement is false. The first one is completed as an example. Give yourself 1 point for each correct answer.

___F___ • Tell only funny stories when trying to make a point.

_______ 1. A story should begin with a quick, interesting sentence.

_______ 2. You should introduce an older person to a younger person.

_______ 3. If you set an appointment correctly, it will not be necessary to verify the date, place, and time of the appointment.

_______ 4. Eye contact is not important in one-to-one conversations.

_______ 5. You should get as close to others as possible when talking.

☞ ***Check your work. Record your score.***

WHAT YOU HAVE LEARNED

- The importance of good listening and speaking skills in your personal life, and the impact which body language can have as you listen and speak.
- How to speak comfortably when beginning a conversation, making introductions, helping others begin conversations, telling a story, setting an appointment, and carrying on a one-to-one conversation.

PUTTING IT TOGETHER

ACTIVITY 6–1 YOUR GOAL: Get 2 or more answers correct.

Fill in the blanks in the space provided as a recall of the Guides for Listening in Conversation. The first one is completed as an example. Give yourself 1 point for each correct answer.

- Look at the speaker with an interested expression________________.

1. Do not fiddle with keys, a pen, or other ________________.
2. Nod, lift your brows, or smile so that the speaker knows you are ________________.
3. Make brief comments or ask ________________ from time to time.

☞ *Check your work. Record your score.*

ACTIVITY 6–2 YOUR GOAL: Get 4 or more answers correct.

Place a T in the space provided if the statement is true. Place an F in the space provided if the statement is false. The first one is completed as an example. Give yourself 1 point for each correct answer.

___T___ • It is important to have an open face when listening.

________ 1. An open face is willing to listen and accept new ideas.

________ 2. A frown shows a willingness to listen.

________ 3. Standing with your arms crossed is a good position for listening.

________ 4. You should choose your conversation topics based on what you like to talk about.

________ 5. Starting a conversation with a good friend is easy.

________ 6. A question is a good way to begin a conversation.

________ 7. A speaker who paces back and forth helps the listener feel more comfortable.

☞ *Check your work. Record your score.*

ACTIVITY 6–3 YOUR GOAL: Get 2 or more answers correct.

For the situations described, write introductions including an icebreaker. Write your answers in the space provided. The first one is completed as an example. Give yourself 1 point for each introduction/icebreaker written.

- Introduce your grandmother to your young next-door neighbor, Akira Matsumi.

  Grandmother, I want you to meet my neighbor, Akira Matsumi. Akira, this is my grandmother Eva Nice. Grandmother Nice will be living with us for the remainder of the summer.

1. You meet the father of your daughter's friend. You introduce yourself.

   ____

   ____

   ____

   ____

2. You are waiting in line at the checkout counter of the local grocery store. Introduce your spouse to your old high school friend, Mike Koch.

   ____

   ____

   ____

   ____

☞ *Check your work. Record your score.*

UNIT 7

POLISHING YOUR SPEAKING SKILLS

WHAT YOU WILL LEARN

When you finish this unit, you will be able to:

- Understand the body parts that enable you to speak.
- Improve your speaking voice by recognizing the importance of the qualities of pitch, volume, tone, and inflection.
- Recognize the importance of correct articulation and pronunciation of words used.
- Add quality to a spoken message by using correct posture, personal appearance, facial expression, and gestures.

WHAT IT TAKES TO SPEAK

Think of speaking as a product. Speaking is a product you market every day. You have the equipment and the know-how to use it. Speaking is the way you communicate and send messages to others. The ability to speak requires that four of your body parts function together. These are the brain, the nervous system, the vocal cords, and the mouth.

Brain

Your brain acts as a computer. The brain scans your available knowledge and sends messages to the nerves to set the muscles into action.

Nervous System

The nervous system activates the muscles so that air is forced up from the lungs. Tiny vocal cords begin moving in the voice box in your throat.

Vocal Cords

Your vocal cords actually vibrate to create the vocal sounds. These sounds are enlarged as they move through your throat, nose, and mouth, and create a voice that is yours alone.

MESSAGES FROM OTHERS

The mind is a wonderful thing—it starts working the minute you're born and never stops—until you get up to speak.

—Anonymous

It takes two to speak the truth . . . one to speak and the other to hear.

—Henry David Thoreau

Mouth

Your mouth shapes the voice into the individual sounds of your speech. Your mouth and tongue move together to shape the words correctly.

These four parts of your body work automatically together to enable you to deliver information to others. Therefore, you can spend your efforts in delivering the best sounding voice possible.

CHECKPOINT 7–1

YOUR GOAL: Get 3 or more answers correct.

Place a T in the space provided if the statement is true. Place an F in the space provided if the statement is false. The first one has been completed as an example. Give yourself 1 point for each correct answer.

___F___ • Your nose shapes the voice into the individual sounds of your speech.

_______ 1. Your body parts work automatically to enable you to speak.

_______ 2. Your vocal cords vibrate to create sounds.

_______ 3. Your brain does not play a part in your ability to speak.

_______ 4. The nervous system activates your muscles so that air is forced into the lungs to allow your vocal cords to produce sounds.

_______ 5. Each voice is different.

☞ ***Check your work. Record your score.***

IMPROVING YOUR SPEAKING VOICE

There is no one right way to speak. Life would be dull if everyone spoke and sounded alike. However, there are certain characteristics of good voice and speech which you should try to apply.

In your effort to deliver a good, clear sounding voice you will need to work to control the pitch, the volume, the tone, the inflection of your voice, and other special voice qualities.

Pitch is the highness or lowness of a voice.

Pitch is the highness or lowness of a voice. The pitch is actually determined by the length, thickness, and tension of your vocal cords. You have no control over the length or thickness of your vocal cords. However, you do have control of the tension. When your vocal cords are too tense, they produce high, squeaky tones. Work at speaking easily and without strain, and your pitch will be pleasant. Ask others, "Is my voice too high or shrill? Is it too low?"

Volume is the loudness or softness of a sound.

Volume is the loudness or softness of a sound. Others will tire quickly of a voice that is too weak and too soft to hear. Have you ever been watching television or listening to the radio that has the volume very low? If you have had this experience, you know what a strain it is to try to hear.

Listening to a very loud voice can also be very annoying. Adjust your voice so that others can hear you clearly without straining. If you are unsure of your volume, ask the help of others. Say, "Am I speaking loudly enough?" or "Am I speaking too loudly?"

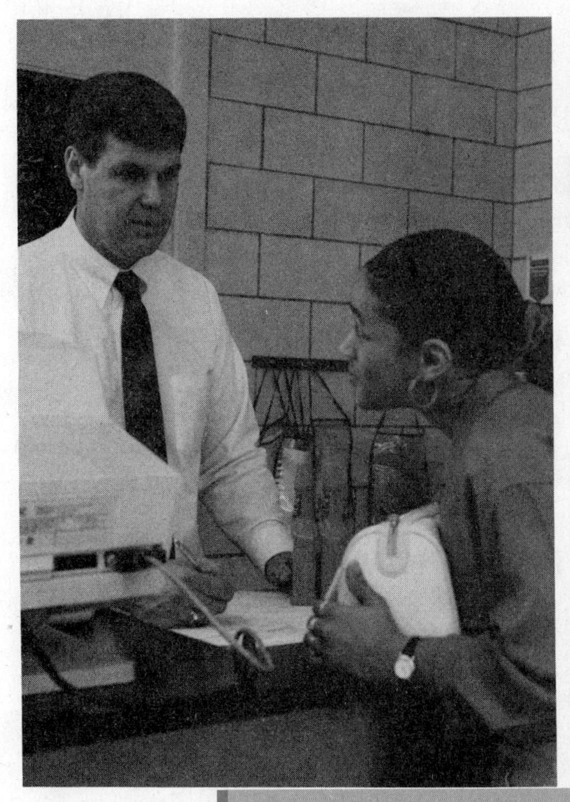

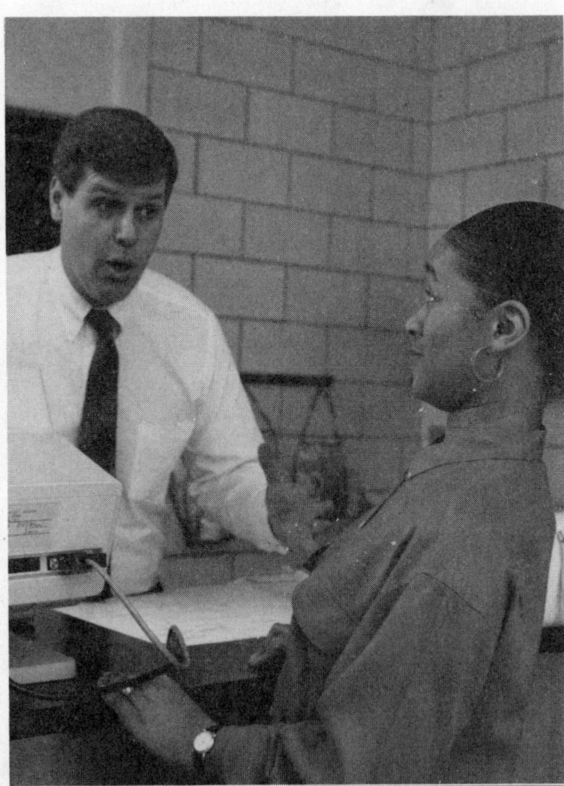

Illustration 7-1
Check your volume.

Tone

Tone is the quality of harshness or smoothness of a sound.

Tone is the quality of harshness or smoothness of a sound. The tone of your voice is the way your voice sounds. There are three sounds in English which should be produced through your nose: *m*, *n*, and *ng*. No other sounds should be produced through the nose. Say this sentence, which has no nasal sounds: "She is outside." Now pinch your nose together and say the sentence again. If you feel no pressure of air through the nose, your tone is probably good. All breath should come through the mouth. If you are unsure of your tone, ask others: "Is my voice clear and pleasing? Do I sound like I am talking through my nose?"

Inflection

Inflection is the rising and falling of your voice.

Monotone is a voice with no expression. It always sounds the same.

Inflection is the rising and falling of your voice. A person who has no inflection speaks in a **monotone**. Your voice should help to express the meaning of words and sentences. Be sure your voice is not always the same. You can do this by changing your pitch, the speed at which you speak, and the volume of your voice according to your meaning. Again, check with others by asking: "Is my voice flat? Does my voice always sound the same?"

CHECKPOINT 7–2

YOUR GOAL: Underline 4 or more subjects correctly.

Read the following groups of sentences aloud. Make your voice express the feelings suggested at the left. Read each line to someone else to check your progress. Give yourself 1 point for each group read effectively.

Feelings	**Sentences**
Interested	1. Are they real diamonds, Ms. Smith? 2. Eiko, did you have a good trip? 3. Did she really win the contest?
Pleasure	1. Sure, I'll help you. 2. What a beautiful fall day this is! 3. Oh, thanks for your help.
Excitement	1. We can go home now, Micaela! 2. The game is over! We won! 3. Frank got the tickets!
Worried	1. That puppy may not have an owner. 2. We haven't seen him for a week. 3. Morris has been ill.

☞ ***Check your work. Record your score.***

MESSAGES FROM OTHERS

The trouble with people who talk too fast is that they often say something they haven't thought of yet.

—Anonymous

Poise is the appearance of being at ease.

—Anonymous

SPECIAL VOICE QUALITIES

In addition to pitch, volume, tone, and inflection, there are other qualities which make your voice easier to understand. These special qualities are articulation and pronunciation.

Articulation

To articulate is to make speech sounds more clearly.

You may become lazy in forming speech sounds. To **articulate** is to make speech sounds more clearly, also called *enunciation.* The main organ of articulation is the tongue. The more carefully you articulate, the more likely you are to be understood. When you articulate or enunciate clearly, you are saying all the letters in every word. Be careful to speak each word clearly and not run words together. For example, avoid the sloppiness of running phrases together like "Havyeetnyet?" Say, "Have you eaten yet?" Also, take care not to leave parts of words unspoken. Say, "breakfast," not "brefast." With a little effort, you can make all of your words clear. In normal rapid speech, *to* may be pronounced *tuh,* and *them* may be pronounced *em.* Say "take them," not "take 'em." Say "had to," not "had tuh."

Be sure to say the *t* and *d* in phrases like "don't you." If you do not, you may end by slurring and saying *choo,* and come out with "donchoo." You should also avoid omitting the *d* or *t* altogether, as in "don'you" or "foun'you," for "don't you" and "found you." If you do not articulate these sounds, your speech is difficult to understand.

CHECKPOINT 7–3

YOUR GOAL: Read 3 groups to someone clearly.

Complete the following exercise with a neighbor, friend, instructor, or family member. Read each group to someone else. Let the other person help you decide how well you are articulating. Give yourself 1 point for each group read clearly.

1. Read aloud the words and make an effort to sound out the italicized consonants clearly.

   *b*uy, ru*b*, *c*ame, *c*ar, ar*c*ti*c*, *d*ay, *g*ame, *l*ow, *m*ay, *m*ine, ra*m*, *n*ice, *p*ear, soa*p*, *s*o, *t*ale, ma*t*, *t*ie, an*t*, ea*t*, *v*eil, *v*i*v*id, *v*ault

2. The italicized letters are often sounded carelessly. Practice saying them aloud. Say the *u* as in *yoo.*

   circ*u*lar particular form*u*la
   ed*u*cation reg*u*lar pop*u*lation

3. Say the long *o.*

   meado*w* shallo*w* yello*w* pillo*w*

4. Be careful to say the *t* in to and the *th* in them.

   see *th*em ought *t*o going *t*o
   trying *t*o try *th*em call *th*e

5. Say the *ing*. Do not omit the sound of *g.*

   do*ing* say*ing* mak*ing*
   go*ing* study*ing* help*ing*
   see*ing* sew*ing* leav*ing*
   hav*ing*

6. Say the *t* and the *d.*

   don'*t* you woul*d* you
   tol*d* you di*d* you

☞ ***Check your work. Record your score.***

Pronunciation

Pronunciation is saying a word correctly.

Articulation is speaking clearly. **Pronunciation** is saying a word correctly. Pronunciation requires that you know what sounds to say when you say a word aloud. If you mispronounce a difficult or unusual word, you are not likely to be criticized. If you mispronounce common words you should know, you make a bad impression or fail to get across your meaning. Good articulation and pronunciation will give you the qualities of a well-spoken person.

If you do not know how to say a word, look it up in a dictionary. Sometimes, when you look up a word, you will find there are two or more ways to pronounce it. The writers of dictionaries consider the first pronunciation the one used more often.

Frequently mispronounced groups of words are listed below. Practice saying these words.

Do not turn around the order of the italicized letters in each of the following words.

Ap*ro*n

Hund*re*d

P*ro*posal

Child*re*n

The vowels in these words are sometimes mispronounced.

Catch (kach). Do not say "kich."

Genuine (jen-yoo-en). Do not say "jen′-ū-īn."

Get (get). Do not say "git."

Maybe (mā′be). Do not say "mebbe."

Just (just). Do not say "jest."

Wrestling (res′ ling). Do not saying "ras′ ling."

Be sure to say the italicized letter in each word:

Reco*g*nize

Congra*t*ulations

Lib*r*ary

Represen*t*ative

Say only the syllables that are a part of each word. Do not add a syllable.

Athlete (ath′ lēt)

Drowned (dround)

Burglar (bur′ gler)

Film (film)

Elm (elm)

Grown (grōn)

CHECKPOINT 7–4

YOUR GOAL: Get 3 or more answers correct.

Look up each of the following words in a dictionary. Decide which one of the pronunciations is most frequently used by careful speakers in your section of the country. Write the word in the space provided the way you think it should be pronounced. The first one is completed as an example. Give yourself 1 point for each correct answer.

- roof **ruf**

1. apricot ____________________
2. pecan ____________________
3. pianist ____________________
4. cheek ____________________

5. greasy ______________________________

☞ ***Check your work. Record your score.***

ADDING QUALITY TO YOUR MESSAGE

After practicing and checking with others to see how you sound, you can think about adding even more quality to what you say by checking your posture, personal appearance, facial expression, and gestures.

Posture

Your posture is important whether you are sitting down or standing up. If you are speaking and want others to pay attention to what you have to say, check your posture. Sit up straight and lean slightly forward as you speak.

If you are standing, stand up straight and distance yourself about 18 inches from the person(s) you are talking to. You probably have found it hard to pay attention to someone who is slouching on a couch or standing with drooping shoulders, or leaning against a wall. This kind of posture does not command attention and respect. The mechanic in Illustration 7-2 is demonstrating both poor and good speaking posture.

Illustration 7-2

Commanding respect with posture.

MESSAGES FROM OTHERS

Tell me, I forget; show me, I remember; involve me, I understand.

—Chinese Proverb

Personal Appearance

How you personally care for yourself sends a message about how you think of yourself. If you want others to hear you, you must give the appearance of self-confidence. Your clothes, your hairstyle, and personal grooming are seen by others as clues to your own self-image. Your personal appearance sends messages about not only how you feel about yourself but also how you relate to others. The old quote from Benjamin Disraeli, "Dress does not make a man, but it often makes a successful one," says it all.

Facial Expression

Your face is very important in sending a message. Usually you read the face of someone who speaks to you. In fact, when you hear the words but cannot see the speaker's face, you may miss the real message being sent. Use your face. If you are sending a happy message, smile. If you are sending a sad message, look unhappy or sad. Help your listener by using your facial expression to help send a message. One study shows a person listening to you gets 7 percent of what you are saying from your words, 38 percent from your voice, and 55 percent from your facial expression. The study results indicate how important facial expression can be.

Gestures

Your hands are very important when used to help send a message. They can emphasize a point, show a size or space (the bear's teeth were this big), show an action (she was wobbly on her feet), or demonstrate something by drawing it in the air. Use your hands to bring meaning to your words.

CHECKPOINT 7–5

YOUR GOAL: Get 3 or more answers correct.

Place a T in the space provided before the true statements. Place an F in the space provided before the false statements. The first one is completed as an example. Give yourself 1 point for each correct answer.

___F___ • Your posture is only important when you are standing and speaking.

_______ 1. Slouching posture commands attention.

_______ 2. Your personal appearance sends messages about how you feel about yourself.

_______ 3. Your personal appearance sends messages about how you relate to others.

_______ 4. Your facial features may say more than your words.

_______ 5. Your hands may bring meaning to your words.

☞ ***Check your work. Record your score.***

WHAT YOU HAVE LEARNED

- The body parts which enable you to speak are: the brain, the nervous system, the vocal cords, and the mouth. They work automatically to give you the product of speech.
- The qualities of pitch, volume, tone, and inflection are necessary if your voice is going to be able to deliver an effective, clear message.
- The importance of correct articulation and pronunciation of words will enable you to be considered well spoken.
- In addition to speaking clearly, it is necessary that your posture, personal appearance, facial expression, and gestures help your voice deliver a message.

PUTTING IT TOGETHER

ACTIVITY 7–1 YOUR GOAL: Get 2 or more answers correct.

Unscramble the important voice qualities in the space provided. The first one is completed as an example. Give yourself 1 point for each correct answer.

- note ___tone___
1. hcipt ______________
2. meovlu ______________
3. niniolftce ______________

☞ *Check your work. Record your score.*

ACTIVITY 7–2 YOUR GOAL: Get 6 or more answers correct.

Place a T in the space provided if the statement is true. Place an F in the space provided if the statement is false. The first one is completed as an example. Give yourself 1 point for each correct answer.

___T___ • Tone is the quality of harshness or smoothness of a sound.

_______ 1. Most sounds in English should be made through the nose.

_______ 2. Inflection is the rising and falling of your voice.

_______ 3. A monotone voice is enjoyable to listen to.

_______ 4. The organ of articulation is the tongue.

_______ 5. Pronunciation is saying a word correctly.

_______ 6. The dictionary shows one way to pronounce each word correctly.

_______ 7. Listening to a very loud voice can be annoying.

_______ 8. There is no one right way to speak.

_______ 9. Pitch is the highness or lowness of a voice.

_______ 10. You have no control over the tension of your vocal cords, which determines the pitch of your voice.

☞ *Check your work. Record your score.*

ACTIVITY 7–3 YOUR GOAL: Get 3 or more answers correct.

Look up each of the following words in a dictionary. Decide which one of the given pronunciations is most frequently used in your section of the country. Write the word the way you think it should be pronounced in the space provided. The first one is completed for you. Give yourself 1 point for each correct answer.

- Potato **pe-tā́t-ō**

1. Juvenile ______________________
2. Iodine ______________________
3. Forehead ______________________
4. Tomato ______________________
5. Aunt ______________________

☞ ***Check your work. Record your score.***

ACTIVITY 7–4 YOUR GOAL: Get 3 or more answers correct.

In the space provided, unscramble the statements about adding quality to your spoken message. The first one is completed as an example. Give yourself 1 point for each correct answer.

- gnidnatS stureop si miropttan.

  Standing posture is important.

1. itS dna nael wardfor sa uoy kaeps.

   ____
2. ooPr erutsop seod ton mmcoand tttaennoi.

   ____
3. alnoserP ppaaeranec ssdne sssmeage.

   ____
4. wSho catnoi thiw ssureteg.

   ____
5. Faacli ssexprieon si miropttna.

   ____

☞ ***Check your work. Record your score.***

UNIT 8
YOUR CHANCE TO SPEAK OUT

WHAT YOU WILL LEARN

When you finish this unit, you will be able to:

- Define and identify the purposes of a speech.
- Develop a speech from an outline.

GIVING A SPEECH

Someday you may have the opportunity to speak to a group of people. You will want to take advantage of this opportunity. Speaking to a group may sound scary. However, if you are well prepared and have something to say, don't allow fear to cause you to turn down the opportunity to share your thoughts with others.

What Is a Speech?

A speech is an occasion when a speaker delivers a message to cause some change in the people who are listening.

There are many possible reasons for giving a speech. A **speech** is defined as an occasion when a speaker delivers a message to cause some change in the people who are listening.

Purposes of a Speech

Each speech has a purpose. Some key purposes follow in Illustration 8-1.

Illustration 8-1

Purposes of a speech.

PURPOSES OF A SPEECH

A speech may be given to:

1. Give information to others.
2. Persuade others to do something.
3. Entertain others.
4. Inspire others.

MESSAGES FROM OTHERS

The tones of human voices are mightier than strings of brass to move the human soul.

—Kropstock

It is good to rub and polish our brain against that of others.

—Montaigne

Give some thought to why you might someday want to give a speech. Do you believe drugs are harmful to young people? Chances are you do. Therefore, wouldn't you like to share your thoughts with young people attending a community meeting. A speech about the harmfulness of drugs would be presented to give information to others. Do you know a lot about a new method used in planting a crop? If so, you could give a speech to inspire others to give the method a try. Do you feel strongly about electing a certain candidate for city or county government? If you do, you could prepare a speech to persuade others to vote for your candidate. Do you know a funny story that would bring joy and laughter to others? You could tell this story in a speech to simply entertain a group of your friends.

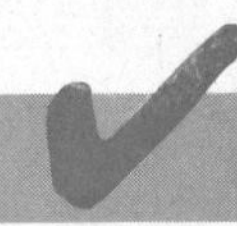

CHECKPOINT 8–1

YOUR GOAL: List 2 or more topics.

In the space provided, list an example topic for each of the purposes for giving a speech. The first one is completed as an example. Give yourself 1 point for each example written.

Purposes for Speeches	Topic
• Give information to others.	• How to Prepare a Special Meal.
1. Persuade others.	1. ______________________
2. Entertain others.	2. ______________________
3. Inspire others.	3. ______________________

Check your work. Record your score.

DEVELOPING A SPEECH

In developing a speech, you will follow three steps. These steps are: selecting the subject, preparing the speech, and delivering the speech.

Selecting the Subject

Sometimes the subject has been selected for you. Or, you have selected the subject based on your own purpose for giving the speech. However, you need to review three rules of selecting the subject to help tailor your subject to the audience and prepare the speech.

Consider the Interests and Needs of the Audience First. The purpose of any speech is to provide information so that the lives of the listeners will change and improve because of what you have shared. Direct your comments, examples, and stories to the audience. Be sure your audience can understand what you are talking about. For example, a speech at a union meeting on who to elect for union steward should include workplace examples and stories directed toward the interest of the audience. Each speech should make the listener feel that you are really talking to him or her. No speech should be given without relating what is being said to the listening audience.

Consider What You Know about the Subject. As you prepare to give a speech, jot down what you know about the subject. There may be areas you are not sure about. You may want to check your facts. You should think about what your audience wants to know. You will want to provide them with new information. Allow yourself time to make a visit to the library, talk to others, and check out facts and information as you prepare to give your speech.

Don't allow yourself to think thoughts like, "Gosh, no one will be interested in what I have to say. I'll just bore them." If you examine the interests and needs of your audience, organize your information, and present it with enthusiasm, your audience will be interested and will learn something from you.

Do Not Make Your Topic Too Broad. You want to be able to cover the topic in the time you have been given. For example, the topics "Food," "Automobiles," or "Gardening" are too broad. Break the topic into a manageable piece. "My Favorite Chinese Food," "The Car I Drive," or "How to Grow Petunias" would be topics to present in a short period of time. Remember the mind can only absorb what the seat can endure.

Illustration 8-2

Researching your subject

CHECKPOINT 8–2

YOUR GOAL: Get 2 or more answers correct.

In the space provided, list the three rules of selecting the subject presented in this unit. Give yourself 1 point for each correct answer.

1. ____________________

2. ____________________

3. ____________________

Check your work. Record your score.

Preparing the Speech

The preparation of the speech may be tough. Keep in mind that good preparation means success. Follow the steps of preparation with care.

1. Decide the specific purpose of your speech. Review the general purposes listed in Illustration 8-1. If you decide what it is you wish to tell the listener and why you wish to tell them, the rest of the organizing will be easier.

2. Use an outline to organize your speech. The speech outline has three major parts: introduction, body, and conclusion.

Introduction. You will first want to get the attention of your audience. There are many ways to do this: use an example, tell a story, use a shocking statement, or use a series of interesting facts.

Body. The body is simply telling the audience what it is you want them to know. The best way to tell the audience what you want them to know is to organize your information into logical points.

Conclusion. At the end of the speech, you will give a brief review of what has been said and tell the audience how what you have said will impact on them. The conclusion will be your last chance at getting your message across. There are several plans you may want to consider. You might use a personal example that shows the audience how valuable your information has been to them. You could tell a joke which shows the value of the information. You might repeat a portion of your opening sentence, to give your listener the feeling of having heard a complete speech. Or you could use a bold statement that shows the audience what will happen if it does not use the information given.

Now all you need to do is fill in the points you want to make within the outline. For example, suppose you have been asked by your community group to talk about "Living in a Large Family." Your outline might look something like this:

LIVING IN A LARGE FAMILY

I. Introduction—Short story about how mealtime can be a circus.

II. Body

A. Attention from brothers and sisters

B. Sharing attention from parents

C. Space planning

D. Sharing chores

III. Conclusion—Review the positive points and joys of a large family. Encourage others to see how the joy of a large family outweighs the worries about money, space, and other hardships.

The best way to write your outline notes is on index cards, as shown in Illustration 8-3. The cards can be easily held in your hand. You will want to write out and memorize the first and

Illustration 8-3

Speech outline.

last sentence of your talk. You should choose the exact wording of the rest of the talk while you are speaking. Then you won't need to keep your eyes glued to your notes, and your talk will sound lively. Of course, you will have spent some planning time carefully thinking through what it is you want to present.

CHECKPOINT 8–3

YOUR GOAL: Write an introduction.

Review the outline in Illustration 8-3. Write an introduction for that speech in the space provided. Give yourself 1 point for writing an introduction.

____

____

____

____

____

Check your work. Record your score.

Deliver the Speech

Certainly the key to making a good speech is to have something interesting to say and to say it well and naturally. If you are nervous, practice your talk aloud at home. You may want to practice before a mirror. Give your speech to members of your family or friends. Then, when you are giving the speech before a larger group, imagine that you are talking to a friend.

When your opportunity to speak comes, walk quickly, forcefully, and confidently to the front of the room and wait quietly for everyone's attention before you begin. Look at the audience, smile, take a deep breath, and then begin to share your thoughts and ideas.

As you present your speech, keep in mind that you must be heard. You will need a pleasant voice with volume. If you speak to the people in the back of the room, your voice will be heard. You will loose your audience in a hurry if they cannot hear what you are saying.

Sometimes, as you are talking, you may find yourself stuck for a word or thought. If this happens, glance down at your notecards, think about what you have just said, and just wait until the word or thought comes. Do not fill in the time with "uh, uh . . ." Do not apologize to the audience if you get stuck. Just go on with the speech. Don't allow your body to detract from what you are saying.

Illustration 8-4

Practicing a speech.

Avoid meaningless and repeated gestures like scratching your head or pulling on your ear. Don't lean against a speaking podium or wall. Stand on both feet and don't rock from foot to foot. Examples of these distracting motions are shown in Illustration 8-5.

Illustration 8-5

These body motions will be speaking so loudly your audience will not be able to hear.

MESSAGES FROM OTHERS

If you can't write your idea on the back of my calling card, you don't have a clear idea.

—David Belasco

Speak kind words, and you will hear kind echoes.

—Anonymous

Look mainly at your listeners. Glance only as you need to at your notes. Pick out four or five people in different parts of the room and speak to them, shifting your eyes from one to another.

Your speech may be supported by an exhibit, picture, or some other illustration. You may want to sketch or write some things on a chalkboard. If you choose, to support your words with these types of aids, don't forget you are talking to the audience. If an aid overwhelms the speech or draws constant attention to itself, it's not a good aid and should not be used.

As you approach the end of the speech, don't drift away with declining volume or lack of force. Give them your last line with force. Smile. Sit down. Don't end with, "I guess that's it," or "That's all I have to say," or "I can't think of anything else."

CHECKPOINT 8–4

YOUR GOAL: Get 4 or more answers correct.

Place a T in the space provided if the statement is true. Place an F in the space provided if the statement is false. The first one is completed as an example. Give yourself 1 point for each correct answer.

___F___ • A good line to end a speech would be "That's all I have to say."

________ 1. Practice is not necessary if you have given adequate thought to preparing a speech.

________ 2. Wait for everyone's attention before beginning a speech.

________ 3. Adjust the volume of your voice so that you are talking to the audience in the front row.

________ 4. You should apologize to the audience if you get stuck for a word or thought.

_______ 5. Avoid scratching your head or making other meaningless gestures as you speak.

_______ 6. Avoid looking at your audience.

_______ 7. A smile at the beginning and ending of a speech is appropriate.

☞ ***Check your work. Record your score.***

WHAT YOU HAVE LEARNED

- The purpose of a speech may be to give information to others, persuade others, entertain others, or to inspire others.
- A good speech is constructed by preparing an outline which will include an introduction to get the attention of the audience, a body of information you want to share with the audience, and a conclusion, which will review what the audience has been told and how the information will impact them.

PUTTING IT TOGETHER

ACTIVITY 8–1 YOUR GOAL: Get 2 or more answers correct.

In the space provided, give the purpose of the speech topic described in the left column. The first one is completed as an example. Give yourself 1 point for each correct answer.

Topic	Purpose of Speech
• How to Make Bread	Give information to others
1. Vote for Joe Smith for City Council	______
2. A Summer Vacation to Remember	______
3. Feel Better About Yourself	______

☞ *Check your work. Record your score.*

ACTIVITY 8–2 YOUR GOAL: Get 3 or more answers correct.

Place a T in the space provided if the statement is true. Place an F in the space provided if the statement is false. The first one is completed as an example. Give yourself 1 point for each correct answer.

___F___ • All speeches are written to entertain.

______ 1. Check your facts before presenting them.

______ 2. No topic is too broad for a speech.

______ 3. You will always get to select the subject for your speech.

______ 4. You should consider the interests and needs of the audience you are speaking to.

______ 5. The purpose of any speech is to provide information that will change and improve the lives of the audience.

☞ *Check your work. Record your score.*

ACTIVITY 8–3 YOUR GOAL: Get 2 or more answers correct.

In the space provided, list the purpose of the three parts of the speech.

Introduction: ______

______

______

____

Body: ______________________________

____

____

Conclusion: ______________________________

____

____

____

☞ *Check your work. Record your score.*

ACTIVITY 8–4 YOUR GOAL: Get 3 or more answers correct.

Place an X in the space provided if the statement is a good speaking habit. Place an O in the space provided if the statement is a poor speaking habit. The first one is completed as an example. Give yourself 1 point for each correct answer.

___O___ • Rocking back and forth while speaking.

_______ 1. Using notecards.

_______ 2. Taking a deep breath before beginning a speech.

_______ 3. Talking to the people in the back row.

_______ 4. Leaning against the podium.

_______ 5. Looking at the audience.

☞ *Check your work. Record your score.*

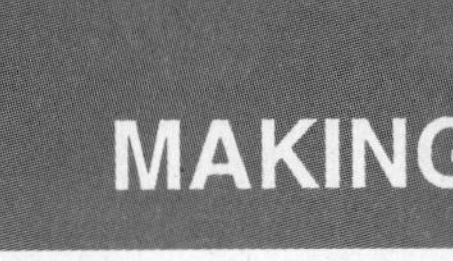

MAKING IT WORK

REVIEW III–1 YOUR GOAL: Get 5 or more correct.

Match the terms in Column A with the definitions in Column B. Write the correct letter in the space provided. The first one is completed as an example. Give yourself 1 point for each correct answer.

- __B__ Persuasion
1. _____ Inflection
2. _____ Pitch
3. _____ Icebreaker
4. _____ Tone
5. _____ Volume
6. _____ Monotone
7. _____ Human being

A. The loudness or softness of a sound.

B. The attempt to get others to adopt or agree with an idea that you have.

C. The highness or lowness of a voice.

D. A voice with no expression.

E. One who is able to work, love, play, and communicate with others.

F. The rising and falling of a voice.

G. The harshness or smoothness of a sound.

H. A topic that helps to start a conversation.

☞ ***Check your work. Record your score.***

REVIEW III–2 YOUR GOAL: Get 8 or more correct.

Complete the following sentences in the space provided using the words listed below. The first one is completed as an example. Give yourself 1 point for each correct answer.

- An open face means a face willing to listen and accept new __ideas__.

1. Starting a conversation with a good friend is ______________.
2. A good technique to use in starting a conversation is to ask a ______________.
3. Your body language can take away the meaning of your spoken ______________.
4. Your vocal cords actually vibrate to create the vocal ______________.
5. Pronunciation is saying a word ______________.
6. Your clothes, hairstyle, and personal grooming are seen by others as clues to your own ______________.

7. A major part of your speaking on the job will be sharing with and providing information to ____________________.

8. Avoid expressions like "It was very funny" when telling a ____________.

9. If you are sending a happy message, ____________________.

10. A story should begin with a quick, interesting ____________________.

Correctly, Easy, Ideas, Message, Others, Question, Self-image, Sentence, Smile, Sounds, Story

☞ *Check your work. Record your score.*

REVIEW III–3 YOUR GOAL: Get 6 or more correct.

Place a T in the space provided if the statement is true. Place an F in the space provided if the statement is false. The first one is completed as an example. Give yourself 1 point for each correct answer.

- __F__ A person listening to you gets 99 percent of your message from your words.

1. ______ Each voice is different.
2. ______ If you set an appointment correctly, it will not be necessary to verify the date, place, and time of the appointment.
3. ______ An icebreaker should be offered as a part of an introduction.
4. ______ Do not look at a speaker as he or she is speaking.
5. ______ The introduction of a speech should get the attention of the audience.
6. ______ Tell only funny stories when trying to make a point.
7. ______ The pitch of a voice is the loudness or softness.
8. ______ Sounds other than the *m*, *n*, and *ng* should not be produced through the nose.

☞ *Check your work. Record your score.*

REVIEW III–4 YOUR GOAL: Get 8 or more correct.

Complete the following activities in the space provided. Give yourself 2 points for each completed activity.

1. Write the opening lines of a speech to present how to use a copy machine.

2. Introduce a neighbor who is a senior citizen to a young person who has just moved into the apartment building where you live.

3. Write a line to start a conversation with someone you are introduced to at a party.

4. Write the three main parts of a speech and explain the purpose of each part.

5. Write what you would say to introduce yourself to a new co-worker you see at the time clock.

____

____

____

____

____

☞ ***Check your work. Record your score.***

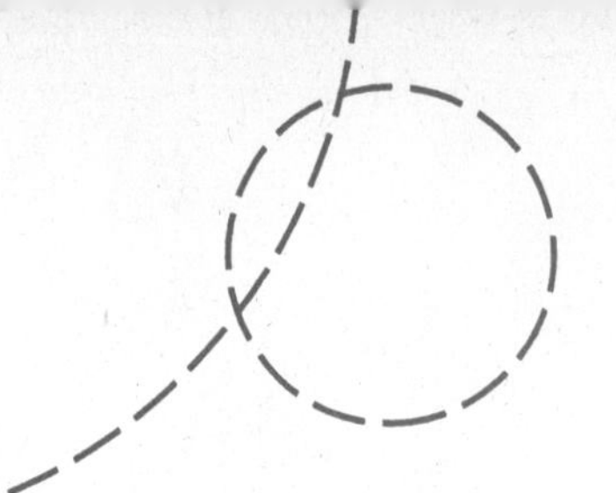

GLOSSARY

A

Active listener. A person who works at listening to learn from others.

Articulate. To make speech sounds more clearly. Also called *enunciation*.

C

Channel. The route which a message takes to get to the receiver.

Communication. The process of sending and receiving information.

Critical listener. A person who listens to determine the accuracy of the message.

Customer. A person who buys a product or service from you or the business organization you work for.

D

Defensive listener. A person who is not willing to listen to anything that does not agree with his or her beliefs.

E

Emotional listener. A person who is overwhelmed by feelings upon hearing a certain word or words.

F

Fact. A statement that can be proven.

Facts listener. A person who does not want to hear back ground information or listen to any more information than necessary.

Feedback. The actions of the receiver of a message.

H

Human being. One who is able to work, love, play, and communicate with others.

I

Icebreaker. A topic that helps to start a conversation.

Inflection. The rising and falling of your voice.

L

Lazy listener. A person who listens only enough to get by.

M

Message. The item of communication that is sent or received.

Monotone. A voice with no expression. It always sounds the same.

N

Nonverbal message. A message sent without using words.

O

Opinions. Statement based on personal beliefs or feelings.

P

Persuasion. The attempt to get others to adopt or agree with an idea that you have.

Pitch. The highness or lowness of a voice.

Pronunciation. Saying a word correctly.

S

Selfish listener. A person who listens only to what he or she wants to hear as it relates to his or her wants, needs, or views.

Speech. An occasion when a speaker delivers a message to cause some change in the people who are listening.

Supervisor. A person who directs and inspects the work of several people in a work area.

T

Tone. The quality of harshness or smoothness of a sound.

V

Verbal message. A message sent using words.

Volume. The loudness or softness of a sound.

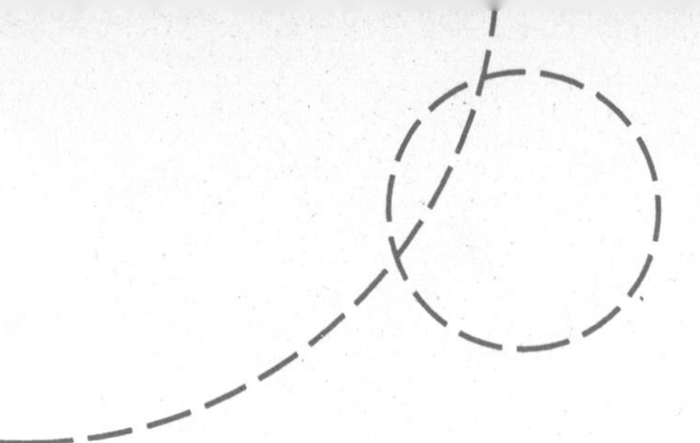

INDEX

L

M

N

O

P

R

S

T

V

W

ANSWERS

UNIT 1

CHECKPOINT 1–1, PAGE 5

Sample answers:

List two messages or sounds most often heard in the city.

1. Traffic noises.
2. Roar of a truck.

List two messages or sounds received from someone today.

1. The message to call a friend.
2. Directions to a doctor's office.

List two messages or sounds you like to receive in the country.

1. The soft "moo" of a cow.
2. The chirp of a robin.

CHECKPOINT 1–2, PAGE 6

Sample answers:

List four messages which give information that you have sent today.

1. Told your child to go to school.
2. Offered to work overtime.
3. Told a friend how to find the Social Services office.
4. Told a neighbor the bus fare to downtown.

List four warnings you have given today or in the past.

1. Don't go into the water for two hours after eating.
2. Watch out for the person on the motorcycle!
3. The dog bites!
4. Stay inside the safety lines.

Write out a direction you have given or plan to give today.

1. Send the rent check to the landlord. The address is 1415 Winter Street, Lincoln, NE 68506-1415. The checkbook is in the top drawer in the kitchen cabinet next to the sink. A stamp and envelope are on top of the refrigerator.
2. Joel lives on Spring Street. Stay on the north side of the street and walk down to the first light. Turn to your right and walk one block to Spring Street. Joel's house is white with green trim and has a chain-link fence.

CHECKPOINT 1–3, PAGE 8

Your answers may vary. Nonverbal messages do not mean the same thing to everyone.

1. Tense or a nervous person. Perhaps annoyed about something.
2. Excited about something. Mad about something and showing anger.
3. Tense. Anticipating something that is about to happen.
4. Defensive mood. Unhappy about something. Not open to suggestion.
5. Giving sharp, accusing directions.

CHECKPOINT 1–4, PAGE 11

	Sight	Sound	Touch
1.			X
2.			X
3.		X	

ACTIVITY 1–1, PAGE 12

There are no specific answers in the activity. Did you review the cartoon to find a sender and a listener? Did you notice that many cartoons are funny because the circle of communication is not complete?

ACTIVITY 1–2, PAGE 12

There are no specific answers. A sample of five is listed.

1. Shaking a fist
2. Pulling on an ear
3. Rubbing the nose
4. Frowning
5. Winking

ACTIVITY 1–3, PAGE 13

Your answers may vary. Compare your answers with someone else after the activity is complete.

1. The man has been skiing and broke his leg.
2. The woman is poor and homeless.
3. The student is tired or uninterested.
4. It is the Fourth of July.
5. A loved one is ill or has died.

UNIT 2

CHECKPOINT 2–1, PAGE 15

There is no specific key to this exercise; sample answers are listed. Have a fellow student, a friend, or a co-worker go over the work with you.

1. Noise of shuffling bulletins or papers; turning pages in songbooks
2. Crying child
3. Street sounds—sirens, cars passing, horns honking
4. Squeeky door
5. Children playing
6. People talking
7. Furnace or air-conditioning noises
8. Someone leaving the room

CHECKPOINT 2–2, PAGE 17

1. Noise
2. Poor attitude
3. Thinking ahead
4. Mind moving too fast
5. Lack of attention

CHECKPOINT 2–3, PAGE 19

There is no specific key to this exercise; sample answers are listed. Review your work with a fellow student, a friend, or a co-worker.

1. Democrat
2. Nerd
3. Gay
4. Honky
5. Jesus Freak

CHECKPOINT 2–4, PAGE 20

1. Emotional listener
2. Facts listener or lazy listener
3. Defensive listener or selfish listener
4. Lazy listener
5. Poor attitude

ACTIVITY 2–1, PAGE 25

1. Lack of attention
2. Thinking ahead
3. Poor attitude
4. Noise
5. Mind moving too fast

ACTIVITY 2–2, PAGE 25

1. Selfish
2. Lazy
3. Emotional
4. Facts
5. Defensive

ACTIVITY 2–3, PAGE 26

1. A
2. E
3. D
4. F
5. B
6. C

ACTIVITY 2–4, PAGE 26

1. Fact
2. Opinion
3. Opinion
4. Fact
5. Opinion

UNIT 3

CHECKPOINT 3–1, PAGE 30

PROFESSIONAL FOOTBALL ON TELEVISION

Date: Current
Time: Current

I. Professional football and television
   Football players big stars
   Football big business
II. Major network support
   NBC—American Conference
   CBS—National Conference
   ABC—Monday night games of both conferences
III. Televised football is fun
   Close camera action
   Announcers explain plays
   Color brings to life

CHECKPOINT 3–2, PAGE 31

SPRAYING VEGETABLES

Date: Current
Time: Current

Spray the vegetables at 9:00 a.m. Hoses are under the lettuce bin. Put the hose in No. 2 position for spraying. Spray all vegetables until they are wet. See Su-ling for questions.

CHECKPOINT 3–4, PAGE 36

Give yourself 1 point for each line correctly completed.

CHECKPOINT 3–3, PAGE 32

CONSUMER PROBLEMS AFFECT EVERYBODY

Date: Current
Time: Current

1. Don't be overwhelmed by advertising.	Check with others.
2. Watch out for emotional, judgment words and expressions.	*Free, Bonus, Giant, Economy.*
3. Check labels.	
4. Read the contents of food.	
5. Guard against your weaknesses.	Shopper beware!

Telephone Message

For Jane — From Cristina Mendez

Would like you to call [X] — Left no message [ ]

Returned your call [ ] — Will call again [ ]

Left the following message: The number is a neighbor who will call her to the phone.

Tel. number 555-8167 Date Current Time Current By Initials

CHECKPOINT 3–5, PAGE 37

Date: Current Time: Current

—Call Ralph at 555-8167, extension 421, as soon as possible.
—Go to work one hour early tomorrow.
—You are first on overtime list.
—Needs an answer.
—Rex.

CHECKPOINT 3–6, PAGE 38

1. No, I said I wanted to go to the plant.
2. Yes, I would like to go with you to the community center.
3. It costs 65 cents to ride to the city center.
4. Yes, I agree with you.
5. Great. I have one daughter.

ACTIVITY 3–1, PAGE 40

STATUS SYMBOLS

Date: Current
Time: Current

I. Status symbols
   Purchase to impress others
   Value created by someone else
   Expensive car example of status symbol
II. False symbols
   Symbol may cause financial difficulty
   False impression created by symbol
   Symbols more important than what is real
III. Think before you buy

ACTIVITY 3–2, PAGE 40

JOB AT THE OASIS

Date: Current
Time: Current

There is a job opening at the Oasis Restaurant for the hours of 7:00 a.m. to 1:30

p.m. The opening is for someone to operate the cash register and seat customers. The restaurant is on 12th and Broadway. The No. 1 Broadway bus goes near the restaurant. Get off the bus at 10th and Broadway. Walk two blocks north.

ACTIVITY 3–3, PAGE 42

1. C
2. A
3. B
4. E
5. D

ACTIVITY 3-4, PAGE 42

Telephone Message

For Edith From Dr. Craig's Office

Would like you to call [X] Left no message [ ]

Returned your call [ ] Will call again [ ]

Left the following message Before noon call Dr. Craig's office to reschedule a dentist appointment

Tel. number 555-8168 Date Current Time Current By Initials

ACTIVITY 3-5, PAGE 43

1.	________ ________	Correct: Date:______ Time:______
2.	Call Elijah Wather	Correct: Call Ivan Wather
3.	Old-age benefits	Correct: Disability benefits
4.	555-7534	Correct: 555-7543
5.	someone named Ivan	Correct: son named Elijah Wather

MAKING IT WORK

REVIEW I–1, PAGE 44

1. T	6. T	11. T	16. T
2. F	7. T	12. T	17. T
3. T	8. T	13. F	18. F
4. F	9. T	14. F	19. F
5. T	10. T	15. T	20. T

REVIEW I–2, PAGE 45

1. D
2. A
3. B
4. E
5. F

REVIEW I–3, PAGE 45

1. sender
2. message
3. receiver
4. feedback

REVIEW I–4, PAGE 46

Today's date (1)
Time (2)
Martha (3)
Please call Susie Michael (4) at the Brownville Community Center (5). Her number is 555-3827 (6). When you call her, please have your social security number handy (7). Important that she talk with you today. (8)

Doug (9)

UNIT 4

CHECKPOINT 4–1, PAGE 50

1. Where are the stocking shelves?
2. May I repeat that information so I am sure that I understand correctly?
3. Are the stockroom and the storeroom the same place?
4. Are the aisles and shelves marked?
5. Do we sell women's shoes?
6. Could we take a look at the stockroom?

CHECKPOINT 4–2, PAGE 52

Give yourself 1 point for each correct answer.

	Work Time	Break/Lunch Time
1.	X	
2.	X	
3.		X
4.		X
5.	X	
6.	X	
7.		X

CHECKPOINT 4–3, PAGE 54

There are no specific answers to this exercise. Sample reasons are given below:

1. Explain a new piece of equipment.
2. Review rules about using the parking lot.
3. Explain a new company fitness plan.
4. Introduce new workers or supervisors.
5. Give an annual report about the progress of the company.

CHECKPOINT 4–4, PAGE 56

Telephone Message

For *Pat Drake* From *Duane*

Would like you to call ☐ Left no message ☐

Returned your call ☐ Will call again ☐

Left the following message *Greater Freight will deliver our vegetable order No. 54839 at 1:25 p.m.*

Tel. number ______ Date *Current* Time *1⁰⁰ pm* By *Michi*

CHECKPOINT 4–5, PAGE 58

1. X
2. O
3. O
4. X
5. O

ACTIVITY 4–1, PAGE 61

1. Which invoice?
2. Who was the shipper?
3. Will you show me the mistakes?

ACTIVITY 4–2, PAGE 61

1. X
2. X
3. O
4. X
5. O

ACTIVITY 4–3, PAGE 62

1. X
2. O
3. X
4. O
5. X

ACTIVITY 4–4, PAGE 62

1. "I don't know. Let's talk about it over coffee."
2. "Sounds good. Tell me about it at lunch."
3. OK
4. "I'll have to think about it. We can talk about it at break."
5. OK

UNIT 5

CHECKPOINT 5–1, PAGE 65

1. be
2. provide/give
3. saying
4. control
5. clearly

CHECKPOINT 5–2, PAGE 67

1. F
2. T
3. T
4. T
5. T
6. F
7. T
8. T

CHECKPOINT 5–3, PAGE 70

1. questions
2. requests
3. explain
4. attempt
5. story

CHECKPOINT 5–4, PAGE 72

There are no specific answers to this exercise. Some possible answers are given below:

1. I have been a stock clerk in the produce department for a large grocery store.
2. I enjoy working outdoors very much. This is one of the reasons I am seeking employment with the forestry service.
3. I could begin working for the forestry service after giving a two-week notice to my present employer.
4. I would be successful because I love the outdoors and I am concerned about the future of our environment.
5. I would be willing to travel if the position requires it.

CHECKPOINT 5–5, PAGE 74

1. Listen carefully.
2. Ask questions to clarify the concerns.
3. State your side of the story.
4. Indicate that you will work to improve.
5. Thank the reviewer for his or her time.

ACTIVITY 5–1, PAGE 76

1. X You were willing to help Meredith. You were looking for more information to help her.
2. O You did not ask if Ileana understood the directions.
3. O Your answer was appropriate, but you used the opportunity to begin a nonwork-related conversation.

ACTIVITY 5–2, PAGE 77

There are no specific answers to this exercise. Here are some sample answers:

1. Did you know this ice cream is low in calories?
2. Do you remember the hours I filled in for you so that you could attend your son's graduation?

3. I didn't like the new idea either until Joe showed me how much time I could save.
4. Do you know that Slide Soap is used in the White House?

ACTIVITY 5–3, PAGE 78

There are no specific answers to this exercise. Some possible answers are given below:

1. Why do you want to work here?
2. I would like to work here because of the pleasant working conditions and fair wages.
3. How can I improve my work?

MAKING IT WORK

REVIEW II–1, PAGE 79

There are no specific answers to this exercise. Here are some sample answers:

1. Story about a cute trick done by your dog.
2. Marital problems.
3. Problems with your teenager.
4. A personal medical concern.
5. Problem with your boyfriend or girlfriend.

REVIEW II–2, PAGE 79

1. Listen carefully.
2. Ask questions.
3. Try out the procedure.
4. Ask for feedback.
5. Repeat the procedure.

REVIEW II–3, PAGE 79

1. T
2. F
3. F
4. T
5. T
6. F
7. T
8. T
9. F
10. T

REVIEW II–4, PAGE 80

There are no specific answers to this exercise. Some sample answers are given below:

1. Ask: Marge, will you answer my telephone for about 10 min utes? I need to help the new employee.
   Explain: I need to show the new em ployee how to operate the lathe.
   Appreciation: I sure would appreciate your help.
2. My neighbor called and said, "Wow! How can you afford a new car?" I was confused. I said, "I didn't get a new car." Then I realized what had happened. The neighbor thought my newly waxed car was new.
3. a. My experience with animals other than dogs and cats has been limited. I have had the opportunity a few times to care for a neighbor's pet canary.
   b. Many questions need to be asked in matching a pet to an owner. I would ask questions about the prospective owner's life-style, questions about the prospective owner's expectations of a pet, and questions about previous pet ownership.

UNIT 6

CHECKPOINT 6–1, PAGE 86

There are no specific answers to this exercise. Two possible answers are listed.

1. Mary seems sympathetic to my problems.
2. Fred always tells funny stories.

CHECKPOINT 6–2, PAGE 89

There are no specific answers to this exercise. Your answers may be similar to the following:

1. Basketball: Did you watch the NBA playoffs?
2. Your children: Let me tell you what happened to my daughter this week.
3. Weather: Are you enjoying this warm weather?
4. Television: Did you watch last night's episode of "Cheers?"

CHECKPOINT 6–3, PAGE 92

1. Good morning. I am (your name). What is your name? Have you been a member here long?
2. Guy, I would like you to meet a friend of mine, Sharon Meyer. Sharon, this is Guy Ingles. Guy's hometown is Hunterville, too.

CHECKPOINT 6–4, PAGE 94

1. T
2. T
3. F
4. F
5. F

ACTIVITY 6–1, PAGE 95

1. objects/things
2. listening
3. questions

ACTIVITY 6–2, PAGE 95

1. T
2. F
3. F
4. F
5. T
6. T
7. F

ACTIVITY 6–3, PAGE 96

1. Mr. Smith, I am (your name). Our daughters are friends. They play well together, don't they?
2. Gail, I want you to meet Mike Koch. Mike, this is my wife, (her name). Mike and I went to high school together.

UNIT 7

CHECKPOINT 7–1, PAGE 98

1. T
2. T
3. F
4. T
5. T

CHECKPOINT 7–2, PAGE 100

There is no specific key to this exercise. Read each group of sentences to someone twice.

CHECKPOINT 7–3, PAGE 101

Read each group of words to someone else.

CHECKPOINT 7–4, PAGE 103

1. ap´-re-kät
2. pi´-kän
3. pē-an´-est
4. chēk
5. grē-sē

CHECKPOINT 7–5, PAGE 105

1. F
2. T
3. T
4. T
5. T

ACTIVITY 7–1, PAGE 107

1. pitch
2. volume
3. inflection

ACTIVITY 7–2, PAGE 107

1. F
2. T
3. F
4. T
5. T
6. F
7. T
8. T
9. T
10. F

ACTIVITY 7–3, PAGE 108

1. jü´-ve-nīl
2. i´-e-dīn
3. for´-ed
4. te-māt´-ō
5. ant

ACTIVITY 7–4, PAGE 108

1. Sit and lean forward as you speak.
2. Poor posture does not command attention.
3. Personal appearance sends messages.
4. Show action with gestures.
5. Facial expression is important.

UNIT 8

CHECKPOINT 8–1, PAGE 110

There are no specific answers for this exercise. Sample answers are given below:

1. Vote for Olivia Zapata
2. My Dog Can't Do Tricks
3. Give Yourself a Break

CHECKPOINT 8–2, PAGE 112

1. Consider what you know about the subject.
2. Consider the interests and needs of the audience first.
3. Do not make your topic too broad.

CHECKPOINT 8–3, PAGE 114

There are no specific answers for this exercise. Sample answer are given below:

The nation's wildlife population is in danger. Do you care enough to do something about it!

CHECKPOINT 8–4, PAGE 117

1. F
2. T
3. F
4. F
5. T
6. F
7. T

ACTIVITY 8–1, PAGE 119

1. persuade
2. entertain
3. inspire

ACTIVITY 8–2, PAGE 119

1. T
2. F
3. F
4. T
5. T

ACTIVITY 8–3, PAGE 119

Introduction: Part of a speech that is written to get the attention of the audience.
Body: The information you want the audience to know.
Conclusion: Brief review of the speech and the impact it will have on the audience.

ACTIVITY 8–4, PAGE 120

1. X
2. X
3. X
4. O
5. X

MAKING IT WORK

REVIEW III–1, PAGE 121

1. F
2. C
3. H
4. G
5. A
6. D
7. E

REVIEW III–2, PAGE 121

1. easy
2. question
3. message
4. sounds
5. correctly
6. self-image
7. others
8. story
9. smile
10. sentence

REVIEW III–3, PAGE 122

1. T
2. F
3. T
4. F
5. T
6. F
7. F
8. T

REVIEW III–4, PAGE 123

There are no specific answers for this exercise. Some answers are given below:

1. How did we survive before copy machines were invented?
2. Emily Owen, I would like you to meet Sissy Malone. Sissy this is Ms.

Emily Owen. Ms. Owen, Sissy is a new tenant in this building. She lives on the same floor as you do.
3. Do you live in this neighborhood?
4. Introduction: The purpose is to get the attention of the audience.
   Body: Tell the audience what it is you want them to know and why.
   Conclusion: Review what has been said. Tell the audience how what has been said is important to them.
5. Hello, my name is Arnold Overstreet. I have worked here for five years. What is your name?

PERSONAL PROGRESS RECORD

Name: ______________________________

UNIT 1: Communicating with Others

Exercise	Score
Checkpoint 1–1	________
Checkpoint 1–2	________
Checkpoint 1–3	________
Checkpoint 1–4	________
Activity 1–1	________
Activity 1–2	________
Activtiy 1–3	________
TOTAL	________

HOW ARE YOU DOING?	
29 or better	Excellent
24–28	Good
19–23	Fair
Less than 19	See instructor

UNIT 2: Zeroing in on Listening

Exercise	Score
Checkpoint 2–1	________
Checkpoint 2–2	________
Checkpoint 2–3	________
Checkpoint 2-4	________
Activity 2–1	________
Activity 2–2	________
Activity 2–3	________
Activity 2–4	________
TOTAL	________

HOW ARE YOU DOING?	
32 or better	Excellent
27–31	Good
22–26	Fair
Less than 22	See instructor

UNIT 3: Special Listening Skills

Exercise	Score
Checkpoint 3–1	________
Checkpoint 3–2	________
Checkpoint 3–3	________
Checkpoint 3–4	________
Checkpoint 3–5	________
Checkpoint 3–6	________
Activity 3–1	________
Activity 3–2	________
Activity 3–3	________
Activity 3–4	________
Activity 3–5	________
TOTAL	________

HOW ARE YOU DOING?	
30 or better	Excellent
25–29	Good
20–24	Fair
Less than 20	See instructor

PART I: Making It Work

Exercise	Score
Review I–1	________
Review I–2	________
Review I–3	________
Review I–4	________
TOTAL	________

HOW ARE YOU DOING?	
30 or bettter	Excellent
26–29	Good
22–25	Fair
Less than 22	See instructor

UNIT 4: Listening in the Workplace

Exercise	Score
Checkpoint 4–1	______
Checkpoint 4–2	______
Checkpoint 4–3	______
Checkpoint 4–4	______
Checkpoint 4–5	______
Activity 4–1	______
Activity 4–2	______
Activity 4–3	______
Activity 4–4	______
TOTAL	______

HOW ARE YOU DOING?

28 or better	Excellent
23–27	Good
18–22	Fair
Less than 18	See instructor

UNIT 5: Speaking in the Workplace

Exercise	Score
Checkpoint 5–1	______
Checkpoint 5–2	______
Checkpoint 5–3	______
Checkpoint 5–4	______
Checkpoint 5–5	______
Activity 5–1	______
Activity 5–2	______
Activity 5–3	______
TOTAL	______

HOW ARE YOU DOING?

22 or better	Excellent
17–21	Good
12–16	Fair
Less than 12	See instructor

PART II: Making It Work

Exercise	Score
Review II–1	______
Review II–2	______
Review II–3	______
Review II–4	______
TOTAL	______

HOW ARE YOU DOING?

18 or better	Excellent
13–17	Good
8–12	Fair
Less than 8	See instructor

UNIT 6: Everyday Listening and Speaking

Exercise	Score
Checkpoint 6–1	______
Checkpoint 6–2	______
Checkpoint 6–3	______
Checkpoint 6–4	______
Activity 6–1	______
Activity 6–2	______
Activity 6–3	______
TOTAL	______

HOW ARE YOU DOING?

15 or better	Excellent
10–14	Good
5–9	Fair
Less than 5	See instructor

UNIT 7: Polishing Your Speaking Skills

Exercise	Score
Checkpoint 7–1	______
Checkpoint 7–2	______
Checkpoint 7–3	______
Checkpoint 7–4	______
Checkpoint 7–5	______
Activity 7–1	______
Activity 7–2	______
Activity 7–3	______
Activity 7–4	______
TOTAL	______

HOW ARE YOU DOING?	
29 or better	Excellent
24–28	Good
19–23	Fair
Less than 19	See instructor

UNIT 8: Your Chance to Speak Out

Exercise	Score
Checkpoint 8–1	______
Checkpoint 8–2	______
Checkpoint 8–3	______
Checkpoint 8–4	______
Activity 8–1	______
Activity 8–2	______
Activity 8–3	______
Activity 8–4	______
TOTAL	______

HOW ARE YOU DOING?	
19 or better	Excellent
14–18	Good
9–13	Fair
Less than 9	See instructor

PART III: Making It Work

Exercise	Score
Review III–1	______
Review III–2	______
Review III–3	______
Review III–4	______
TOTAL	______

HOW ARE YOU DOING?	
27 or better	Excellent
22–26	Good
17–21	Fair
Less than 17	See instructor